OPPOSING
VIEWPOINTS®
SERIES

Juvenile Crime

Other Books of Related Interest:

Opposing Viewpoints Series

Street Teens

At Issue Series

Guns and Crime

Current Controversies Series

Family Violence

"Congress shall make no law . . . abridging the freedom of speech, or of the press."

First Amendment to the US Constitution

The basic foundation of our democracy is the First Amendment guarantee of freedom of expression. The Opposing Viewpoints series is dedicated to the concept of this basic freedom and the idea that it is more important to practice it than to enshrine it.

OPPOSING VIEWPOINTS® SERIES

Juvenile Crime

Louise I. Gerdes, Book Editor

GREENHAVEN PRESS
A part of Gale, Cengage Learning

GALE
CENGAGE Learning®

Detroit • New York • San Francisco • New Haven, Conn • Waterville, Maine • London

Elizabeth Des Chenes, *Director, Publishing Solutions*

© 2012 Greenhaven Press, a part of Gale, Cengage Learning.

Gale and Greenhaven Press are registered trademarks used herein under license.

For more information, contact:
Greenhaven Press
27500 Drake Rd.
Farmington Hills, MI 48331-3535
Or you can visit our Internet site at gale.cengage.com

For product information and technology assistance, contact us at

Gale Customer Support, 1-800-877-4253
For permission to use material from this text or product, submit all requests online at www.cengage.com/permissions

Further permissions questions can be emailed to permissionrequest@cengage.com

Articles in Greenhaven Press anthologies are often edited for length to meet page requirements. In addition, original titles of these works are changed to clearly present the main thesis and to explicitly indicate the author's opinion. Every effort is made to ensure that Greenhaven Press accurately reflects the original intent of the authors. Every effort has been made to trace the owners of copyrighted material.

Cover Image copyright © Alexander Raths/Shutterstock.com.

LIBRARY OF CONGRESS CATALOGING-IN-PUBLICATION DATA

Juvenile Crime / Louise I. Gerdes, book editor.
    p. cm. -- (Opposing viewpoints)
    Includes bibliographical references and index.
    ISBN 978-0-7377-5731-6 (hardcover) -- ISBN 978-0-7377-5732-3 (pbk.)
    1. Juvenile delinquency--United States. 2. Juvenile justice, Administration of--United States. 3. Juvenile corrections--United States. 4. Gangs--United States. 5. School violence--United States. I. Gerdes, Louise I., 1953-
    HV9104.J8319 2012
    364.360973--dc23

                                                            2012007811

Printed in Mexico
2 3 4 5 6 7 16 15 14 13 12

Contents

Chapter 3: How Should the Criminal Justice System Treat Juvenile Offenders?

Chapter 4: What Policies Will Best Reduce Juvenile Crime?

Why Consider Opposing Viewpoints?

> *"The only way in which a human being can make some approach to knowing the whole of a subject is by hearing what can be said about it by persons of every variety of opinion and studying all modes in which it can be looked at by every character of mind. No wise man ever acquired his wisdom in any mode but this."*
>
> John Stuart Mill

In our media-intensive culture it is not difficult to find differing opinions. Thousands of newspapers and magazines and dozens of radio and television talk shows resound with differing points of view. The difficulty lies in deciding which opinion to agree with and which "experts" seem the most credible. The more inundated we become with differing opinions and claims, the more essential it is to hone critical reading and thinking skills to evaluate these ideas. Opposing Viewpoints books address this problem directly by presenting stimulating debates that can be used to enhance and teach these skills. The varied opinions contained in each book examine many different aspects of a single issue. While examining these conveniently edited opposing views, readers can develop critical thinking skills such as the ability to compare and contrast authors' credibility, facts, argumentation styles, use of persuasive techniques, and other stylistic tools. In short, the Opposing Viewpoints Series is an ideal way to attain the higher-level thinking and reading skills so essential in a culture of diverse and contradictory opinions.

In addition to providing a tool for critical thinking, Opposing Viewpoints books challenge readers to question their own strongly held opinions and assumptions. Most people form their opinions on the basis of upbringing, peer pressure, and personal, cultural, or professional bias. By reading carefully balanced opposing views, readers must directly confront new ideas as well as the opinions of those with whom they disagree. This is not to argue simplistically that everyone who reads opposing views will—or should—change his or her opinion. Instead, the series enhances readers' understanding of their own views by encouraging confrontation with opposing ideas. Careful examination of others' views can lead to the readers' understanding of the logical inconsistencies in their own opinions, perspective on why they hold an opinion, and the consideration of the possibility that their opinion requires further evaluation.

Evaluating Other Opinions

To ensure that this type of examination occurs, Opposing Viewpoints books present all types of opinions. Prominent spokespeople on different sides of each issue as well as well-known professionals from many disciplines challenge the reader. An additional goal of the series is to provide a forum for other, less known, or even unpopular viewpoints. The opinion of an ordinary person who has had to make the decision to cut off life support from a terminally ill relative, for example, may be just as valuable and provide just as much insight as a medical ethicist's professional opinion. The editors have two additional purposes in including these less known views. One, the editors encourage readers to respect others' opinions—even when not enhanced by professional credibility. It is only by reading or listening to and objectively evaluating others' ideas that one can determine whether they are worthy of consideration. Two, the inclusion of such viewpoints encourages the important critical thinking skill of objectively evaluating an author's credentials and bias. This evaluation will illuminate an author's reasons for taking a particular stance on an issue and will aid in readers' evaluation of the author's ideas.

It is our hope that these books will give readers a deeper understanding of the issues debated and an appreciation of the complexity of even seemingly simple issues when good and honest people disagree. This awareness is particularly important in a democratic society such as ours in which people enter into public debate to determine the common good. Those with whom one disagrees should not be regarded as enemies but rather as people whose views deserve careful examination and may shed light on one's own.

Thomas Jefferson once said that "difference of opinion leads to inquiry, and inquiry to truth." Jefferson, a broadly educated man, argued that "if a nation expects to be ignorant and free . . . it expects what never was and never will be." As individuals and as a nation, it is imperative that we consider the opinions of others and examine them with skill and discernment. The Opposing Viewpoints series is intended to help readers achieve this goal.

David L. Bender and Bruno Leone,
Founders

Introduction

"During the closing decades of the twentieth century, juvenile justice policy underwent major change. In less than a generation, a justice system that had viewed most young lawbreakers as youngsters whose crimes were the product of immaturity was transformed into one that [holds] many youths to the same standard of criminal accountability it imposes on adults."

—Elizabeth S. Scott
and Laurence Steinberg,
"Adolescent Development and
the Regulation of Youth Crime,"
Juvenile Justice, Fall 2008.

Throughout history, philosophers and social commentators have complained about the youth of their day. An oft-cited quote attributed by Plato to Socrates of ancient Greece portrays youth as a threat to the social order: "The children now love luxury; they have bad manners, contempt for authority; they show disrespect for elders and love chatter in place of exercise. Children are now tyrants, not the servants of their households." Over the years commentators in the United States have often expressed fears of a coming juvenile crime wave. In 1946, following World War II, congressional representative Henry Ellenbogen warned:

> There is teenage trouble ahead. Plenty of it! We have just won a world war against the Axis enemies. Now we face a new critical war against a powerful enemy from within our gates. That enemy is juvenile delinquency . . . an ever-growing evil, a shocking reality. It is a real and alarming

menace to every city, borough, and township. It is a disease eating at the heart of America and gnawing at the vitals of our democracy.[1]

Public concerns about juvenile crime in the United States have varied in intensity through the years, often influenced by news of particularly shocking crimes. These crimes and the perception of youth as increasingly dangerous to society, however, do not always reflect the actual statistical prevalence of juvenile crime. Nevertheless, they have influenced public opinion and, in turn, public policy. Indeed, a review of the modern history of public perceptions about juvenile crime and developments in juvenile justice in the United States is reflective of the current controversy surrounding how best to protect public safety while also defending the rights of young people.

Prior to a period of extensive social reform in the United States that began in the late nineteenth century, child offenders over the age of seven were imprisoned with adults. In early American history, the criminal justice system treated juvenile criminals no differently than it treated adults. However, Progressive Era reformers believed that children should be rehabilitated rather than punished. In 1899, states began to establish youth reform homes. In that same year, the first juvenile court was established in Cook County, Illinois. The prevailing view was that the state would become the guardian of juveniles who committed crimes—seeing them not as criminals but as children in need of care and direction. Judge Julian W. Mack wrote in a 1907 *Harvard Law Review*:

> Why is it not just and proper to treat these juvenile offenders, as we deal with the neglected children, as a wise and merciful father handles his own children whose errors are not discovered by the authorities? Why is it not the duty of the state, instead of asking merely whether a boy or girl has committed a specific offense, to find out what he is physi-

---

1. Texas Appleseed, *Texas' School-to-Prison Pipeline: Ticketing, Arrest & Use of Force in Schools*, December 2010.

cally, mentally, morally, and then if it learns that he is treading the path that leads to criminality, to take him in charge, not so much to punish as to reform, not to degrade, but uplift, not to crush but to develop, not to make him a criminal but a worthy citizen.[2]

Support for this view spread nationwide, and by 1925 all but two states had established juvenile courts. This paternalistic, rehabilitative model thrived during the first half of the twentieth century. However, the diagnosis and treatment of juvenile delinquency proved less effective than predicted. According to National Center for Juvenile Justice researcher John L. Hutzler, "The failure of the movement to achieve its ultimate objective—the solution to juvenile misbehaviors—eventually began to erode public confidence in the juvenile court."[3]

During the 1960s, public perceptions and juvenile justice policies once again began to change. Policy makers and researchers became concerned about a mounting wave of juvenile crime. Indeed, juvenile arrests had risen at a pace greater than the number of juveniles in the population. Statistics from the period reveal that juveniles were involved in more than 60 percent of car theft arrests, nearly 50 percent of burglary and larceny arrests, 19 percent of forcible rape arrests, 13 percent of aggravated assault arrests, and 8 percent of murder arrests. At the same time that confidence in the rehabilitation and treatment model was eroding, counterculture and civil rights movements that challenged traditional policies and attitudes were growing. By the 1960s, juvenile courts had jurisdiction over nearly all juvenile cases. Unlike criminal trials, these proceedings were informal. Advocates began to complain that youths who faced the loss of their liberty were not afforded the same constitutional protections afforded adults.

2. Julian W. Mack, "The Juvenile Court," *Harvard Law Review 23*, 1907.
3. John L. Hutzler, "Canon to the Left, Canon to the Right, Can the Juvenile Court Survive?," *Today's Delinquent*, July 1982.

The Supreme Court agreed, and several of its decisions gave youths the same constitutional protections as adult criminal defendants. Some commentators claim, however, that these decisions were the first step to moving the juvenile justice system away from its paternalistic role to a model that resembled the adult criminal justice system. In the landmark 1967 case *In re Gault*, a fifteen-year-old boy on probation was accused of making an obscene prank phone call. The Arizona juvenile court decided to confine the boy to the state's reform school until he was twenty-one. The Supreme Court's majority opinion, delivered by Justice Abe Fortas, emphasized that youths were entitled to fair treatment under the law and thus were entitled to the right to receive notice of charges, obtain legal counsel, confront and cross-examine witnesses, and take advantage of the privilege against self-incrimination and appellate review. Prophetically, some claim, Justice Potter Stewart feared that the decision would convert a juvenile proceeding into a criminal prosecution, arguing that the intent of the juvenile justice system was not to prosecute and punish, but to meet society's responsibility to children. In the eyes of some, the juvenile justice policies of the late 1990s would make Justice Stewart's concerns a reality.

During the 1970s, however, the focus on how to address juvenile crime remained rehabilitative but shifted from institutionalization to a focus on prevention. The Juvenile Justice and Delinquency Prevention Act of 1974 created several agencies that remain today—the Office of Juvenile Justice and Delinquency Prevention, which is responsible for implementation of national juvenile justice programs and policies, and the National Institute for Juvenile Justice and Delinquency Prevention, which conducts research and gathers data on juvenile crime. To receive funds made available by the act, states were required to remove youths from correctional facilities and separate them from adults. The belief at the time was that youths became worse when incarcerated with adults, and re-

17

search supported this conclusion. Another goal of the act was to minimize incarceration of youths involved in noncriminal offenses such as curfew violations, truancy, or underage drinking. This view would change dramatically by the late 1990s. Many analysts agree that a convergence of events would lead to the strict juvenile justice policies enacted by most states at the end of the twentieth century.

During a 1978 New York gubernatorial election, a fifteen-year-old named Willie Bosket shot three strangers on a New York City subway platform after having been previously involved with the juvenile justice system. He was sentenced to five years in detention, the maximum sentence he could receive as a juvenile. The highly publicized case led to public outrage over the lenience of juvenile courts that in turn led to a fierce legislative response. New York legislators almost immediately passed the Juvenile Offender Act, which lowered the age of majority for murder to thirteen and to fourteen for other major felonies. This, some analysts assert, led to a major restructuring of the juvenile and criminal court system that was repeated across the nation. This shift was facilitated by a steep rise in juvenile crime that peaked in 1994. Justice Department statistics reveal that juvenile arrests for violent crimes were 40 percent higher than the 24 percent average in previous years. More frightening to many was the revelation that the juvenile arrest rate for murder rose 110 percent from 1987 to 1993.

For critics, what truly stoked the fires of public support for stricter juvenile justice policies were predictions of a coming wave of youth violence forecasted by respected criminologists and policy analysts. In 1995 Northeastern University criminologist James Alan Fox took note of the rise in juvenile arrests for violent crimes in the late 1980s. Based on the anticipated growth in the teen population, he predicted that an influx of violent predatory youth would plague the country after the turn of the century. He recommended juvenile policy shifts to avoid the coming catastrophe. Shortly after, in 1996, Princeton University political science professor John Dilulio more specifically predicted that 270,000 of what he called "superpredators" would hit America's streets by 2010. Although in truth juvenile crime began a dramatic fall in 1995, the idea of a new breed of predatory youth took hold in the media. A January 1996 *Newsweek* headline warned, "Superpredators Arrive." A March 1996 *U.S. News & World Report* cover article, "Teenage Time Bombs," reported that "victims of underage felons [are] challenging the long-standing belief that youngsters who kill, rob and rape should be treated in a different way than adult criminals." By June 1996, legislators were moving to overturn what Fox Butterfield of the *New York Times* reported "has been a fundamental principle of the American juvenile justice system for more than 150 years: the strict separation of jailed young offenders from hardened adult criminals."[4] Indeed, between 1992 and 1997, a total of forty-seven states passed laws making their juvenile justice system stricter. It became easier to transfer juveniles to adult criminal systems and to impose stricter sentences. From 1985 to 1997, the one-day count of state prisoners younger than eighteen rose 135 percent. The average daily population in juvenile detention facilities more than doubled, to twenty-eight thousand.

During this time, youth advocates questioned claims that a wave of violent youth crime would plague the nation. According to Vincent Schiraldi, founder and president of the Justice Policy Institute and past president of the Center on Juvenile and Criminal Justice, the tide of superpredators never arrived. In fact, he claims, youth homicides dropped 68 percent between 1993 and 1999. By 2001, youth crime was at its lowest in twenty-five years. "There would have had to be as many

4. Fox Butterfield, "Republicans Challenge Notion of Separate Jails for Juveniles," *New York Times*, June 24, 1996.

'thugs' under age 6 as over age 13 for the dire warning of 270,000 new 'superpredators' to come true,"[5] Schiraldi asserts. In truth, in 2001 Dilulio retracted his thesis, prompted by this downturn in juvenile crime—the exact opposite of his predictions. Despite these realities, the juvenile justice system has in many states remained punitive, although some states are moving away from incarceration and toward community-based rehabilitative models.

According to youth advocates, studies show that those juveniles transferred to adult court are more likely to be rearrested for violent crime than those handled in juvenile court. Adult prosecution, they argue, is clearly counterproductive. Moreover, claims of widespread physical and sexual abuse and the disproportionate number of minorities in the system add to growing concern that the "get tough" polices of the late 1990s are not just counterproductive but dangerous for America's youth. Youth advocates recommend reduced reliance on incarceration and a return to prevention, rehabilitation, and strict separation of the juvenile and adult criminal justice systems. According to Columbia University law and public health professor Jeffrey Fagan, "While the law has moved toward waiving increasingly younger teens to adult criminal court, social and biological evidence suggests moving in the other direction. Perhaps it's time for the law to change course and follow the science."[6] Despite these calls for reform, some commentators continue to claim that declining juvenile crime rates should not be a signal to change the system. They assert that declining rates demonstrate that these policies are working. According to Minnesota district attorney James C. Backstrom, "when serious crimes are committed by youths,

---

5. Vincent Schiraldi, "Will the Real John Dilulio Please Stand Up," *Washington Post*, February 5, 2001.
6. Jeffrey Fagan, "Juvenile Crime and Criminal Justice: Resolving Border Disputes," *Juvenile Justice*, Fall 2008.

they need to be dealt with appropriately, with significant consequences. If we roll back the clock, we're going to be harming our society."[7]

Clearly, determining the juvenile justice policies that will best protect the rights of America's youth while also protecting society from juvenile crime remains a hotly contested controversy in the juvenile crime debate. The tension between these two competing interests is reflected in many of the viewpoints presented in the following chapters of *Opposing Viewpoints: Juvenile Crime*: Is Juvenile Crime a Serious Problem?, What Are the Causes of Juvenile Crime and Violence?, How Should the Criminal Justice System Treat Juvenile Offenders?, and What Policies Will Best Reduce Juvenile Crime? As state coffers dwindle and juvenile justice programs compete for declining funds, the difficulty for policy makers in reconciling the conflicting needs of youth and public safety will only increase.

7. Peter Katel, "Juvenile Justice," *CQ Researcher*, November 7, 2008.

CHAPTER 1

Is Juvenile Crime a Serious Problem?

Chapter Preface

One of several controversies in the juvenile crime debate is whether juvenile crime is a growing problem. Shocking cases of senseless youth violence tend to spark fears of a youth crime wave. Indeed, the September 24, 2009, beating death of sixteen-year-old honor student Derrion Albert at the hands of five young men aged fourteen to nineteen shocked the nation. The wide circulation of a cell phone video that recorded the assault prompted President Barack Obama to send US Attorney General Eric Holder and Secretary of Education Arne Duncan to Chicago, where the murder took place, to discuss youth violence. In a US Department of Education press release, Holder said, "Youth violence isn't a Chicago problem, any more than it is a black problem or a white problem. It's something that affects communities big and small and people of all races and colors."[1] Statistics show that juvenile crime has declined significantly since its peak in the mid-1990s; in fact, the Justice Department maintains, the murder arrest rate in 2008 was 74 percent lower than in 1983. Nevertheless, when the media report heinous crimes committed by American youth, commentators renew the juvenile crime debate, asking whether youth violence is a growing social concern.

Some experts claim that juvenile crime is not as serious a problem as many Americans believe. Barry Krisberg—former president of the National Council on Crime and Delinquency and senior fellow at the University of California, Berkeley, law school—blames the public perception on the way the media report juvenile crime. In congressional testimony on February 11, 2009, Krisberg cites a study that found media outlets in Dallas, Washington, DC, and San Mateo County, California,

---

1. Press release, "Attorney General and Education Secretary Call for National Conversation on Values and Student Violence," October 7, 2009. www2.ed.gov.

regularly reported increases in juvenile crime, even if short term, and did not report decreases. In addition, he maintains, media attribute violence to youth that is, in fact, committed by young adults. Indeed, says David M. Kennedy, director of the Center for Crime Prevention and Control at John Jay College of Criminal Justice, "People often think this a juvenile issue, but it's not. The offending rate for the 20–24 cohort is consistently much more severe than for actual juveniles." [2]

While most experts do not dispute that juvenile crime is generally on the decline, some argue that the problem nevertheless remains serious in many communities. According to Melissa Sickmund of the National Center for Juvenile Justice, "You can't go into a community that's experiencing a real problem in their world, on their streets, with their kids ending up dead or their kids ending up behind bars because they committed these crimes and tell them nationally stuff is down, it's not a problem."[3] These analysts argue that while aggregate juvenile crime may not be rising, to those living in the community, it can seem that way. "If you're living in a poor, disadvantaged neighborhood with no infrastructure and lots of gang activity, it can seem that [crime] has gotten lots worse in the last couple years,"[4] claims criminologist Jeffrey Butts. Even criminologist Kennedy admits that while overall juvenile crimes have declined, "There remains an extraordinary and unconscionable persistent problem of extremely high violent criminal victimization."[5] He notes, however, that these crimes are generally committed by "a very small population of high-rate offenders involved in high-rate-offending groups like gangs, drug crews, neighborhood sets and so on. . . . Most of

2. Thomas J. Billitteri, "Youth Violence," *CQ Researcher*, March 5, 2010.
3. *Ibid.*
4. *Ibid.*
5. *Ibid.*

the serious violent crime in these communities is perpetrated by members of these standout groups."[6]

Advocates like Northeastern University criminologist James Alan Fox are "still very concerned about what's happening among some Americans in some cities. And I'm concerned that there's very little attention paid toward it because overall things are better."[7] Thus, the debate over the seriousness of juvenile crime, even when faced with statistics showing an overall decline, continues. Commentators on both sides of the issue such as those in the following chapter will continue to inform this debate.

6. *Ibid.*
7. *Ibid.*

> "[There has been] a recent uptick in se-
> verity of juvenile violence in the U.S."

The Severity of Juvenile Crime Is Increasing

Wendy Murphy

Statistics show the brutality of juvenile crimes is increasing, claims Wendy Murphy in the following viewpoint. Murphy argues that with the growing severity of violence, the United States needs a legal system that is tough on juvenile offenders. Citing a recent publication by legal scholars Charles D. Stimson and Andrew M. Grossman on maximum sentencing for juveniles, Murphy offers choice data points and examples of the uptick in juvenile crime. Our challenge, Murphy states, is to find a way to better identify juvenile offenders who can change, instead of wasting taxpayer dollars on juveniles who cannot. Wendy Murphy is a former prosecutor and author of And Justice for Some: An Exposé of the Lawyers and Judges Who Let Dangerous Criminals Go Free.

As you read, consider the following questions:

1. According to the author, why do "anti-incarceration" activists resist LWOP (life without parole) sentences for juveniles?

2. The recent uptick in severity of juvenile violence has prompted states across the country to do what, according to the author?

3. What is one argument the author provides in favor of the option of LWOP for some juveniles?

"Forty-three states, the District of Columbia, and the federal government have set the maximum punishment for juvenile offenders at life without the possibility of parole" (LWOP). So begins a new publication from the Heritage Foundation, where authors . . . Charles [D.] Stimson and [Andrew M. Grossman] argue that juvenile offenders should do "Adult Time for Adult Crimes."

In about 100 pages, Stimson [and Grossman] make a powerful argument that LWOP is an appropriate and just sentence for certain juvenile offenders, and [they] do a stellar job exposing and correcting the record on a surprisingly effective campaign of misinformation, disseminated by "anti-incarceration" activists and gobbled up by the media and policy makers, without regard for the truth or apparent concern for the suffering of victims and the horrific nature of the violence perpetrated by juveniles in this country.

But calling them "anti-incarceration" activists may not be fair. Some of the people who argue against tough punishments for juveniles are fine with incarceration in general as a legitimate law enforcement response to crime, but they hold a sincere belief that kids really can change—and that the bad things they do are less the result of a juvenile's free will than the product of a horrible lifestyle, lack of good parenting and the absence of meaningful and healthy adult relationships. In other words, they resist LWOP sentences not because they're anti-incarceration so much as pro-hope for young offenders.

Juveniles Can Be Capable of Horrific Violence

Whatever the nature of the group pushing the issue, their work should be rooted in facts, not mythical "feel-good" biases that exploit our human desire to believe that a sweet-faced 15-year-old, who looks like the girl or boy next door, is not capable of intentionally killing an innocent human being.

Stimson [and Grossman] also make a strong argument that even those who think juvenile crimes don't affect their lives should care about this issue because certain crimes are so horrific that the idea of a particular offender one day walking free poses too great a risk to civilized society.

For example, a 16-year-old named Ralph David Cruz, Jr. wanted to steal a car when he saw a young mother driving home with her 6-year-old son and 7-year-old daughter in 2001. When she refused, he shot her in the head and chest, then ran over her dead body with the car as he drove away with her kids in the back seat. 30 minutes later, both kids were found dead, execution style, with gunshot wounds to the head. And then there's the story of a 14-year-old offender named Ashley Jones, who anti-LWOP activists have written about by saying she "tried to escape the violence and abuse [in her life] by running away with an older boyfriend who shot and killed her grandfather and aunt." Stimson [and Grossman] provide a more enlightening version of the case by quoting the judge who handled Jones's prosecution: "When Ashley realized her aunt was still breathing, she hit her in the head with a heater, stabbed her in the chest [and] attempted to set her room on fire. . . . As [Ashley's ten-year-old sister] attempted to run, Ashley grabbed her and began hitting her. [Ashley's boyfriend] put the gun in [the little girl's face] and told her that was how she would die. Ashley intervened and said 'No, let me do it,' and proceeded to stab her little sister fourteen times."

Raise your hand if you EVER want Mr. Cruz or Ms. Jones living in your neighborhood.

[The authors'] other case studies make this point over and over again. It's hard to read, actually, but there's no other way to fairly decide whether LWOP is appropriate for certain juveniles without knowing exactly what they did wrong. It isn't an abstract law school question and these are not just "kids" behaving badly. Real human beings lost their lives to grotesque violence at the hands of people who, irrespective of their age, had no capacity to care about human life. Maybe there's an explanation for how they got that way—and we should absolutely spend money understanding the reasons why juveniles kill. But future prevention of other juveniles' violence is not furthered by inadequate response to the violence that's already been done.

Though full of valuable data, [the authors'] statistics aren't always clear. For example, [they] say juveniles in the United States "lead the Western world" in juvenile crime and in one recent year committed as many violent crimes as juveniles in the next seven highest countries combined. This may all well be true, but [they] didn't give out a comparative "per capita" number.

Juvenile Crimes Are Increasingly Severe

Stimson [and Grossman] do include a reference to the U.S. being 14th in murders per capita "committed by youths." And [they] note that when it comes to crime "rates," the U.S. ranks highly in every category, including juvenile crime. Stimson [and Grossman] also note a recent uptick in severity of juvenile violence in the U.S. which has prompted states across the country to lower the age at which juveniles can be transferred to adult court for prosecution. This uptick followed a long period of time during which criminal justice policy centered around a presumption that rehabilitation and not punishment should be the goal of juvenile justice. It would have been helpful to see some data on the relationship between LWOP punishments and a reduction in juvenile violence.

Other data is also relevant—though confusing. For example, Stimson [and Grossman] point out that anti-LWOP activists consistently claim that over 2200 juveniles are serving life without parole sentences in this country, but [they] say that prison officials claim this is a manufactured statistic because it is a virtually impossible number to measure. Even if it's true, is 2200 too many? Stimson [and Grossman] don't say.

Most of us have a soft spot for kids—even when they commit horrible crimes. The younger a child is, the more willing we are to blame the adults around them for the bad things they do. But a soft spot isn't the same as a pass—and when juveniles commit especially violent crimes, the last thing they need is a legal system that sends a message that it's "no big deal."

[The authors'] work dares to say what everyone already knows: too much money is wasted trying to "save" dangerous young people who will never stop hurting others. And while it may seem cynical to have a criminal justice policy that puts this idea [into practice], the real challenge is not to abandon LWOP but to find a way to better identify those young offenders who are truly capable of changing their lives.

Not All Juvenile Offenders Can Change

If we spend precious tax dollars on futile efforts, the kids who really can become productive members of society won't get sufficient resources because there won't be enough money left. We know what sociopathy looks like—in adults and juveniles—and we know it isn't a "fixable" disease. Without the option of LWOP for some juveniles, the criminal justice system will be forced to let even the most dangerous among us kill and kill again, propped up by the romantic and decidedly unscientific hope that change is always possible.

[The authors'] final argument about international law is powerful—and should easily prevail against any claim that the United States is somehow legally compelled by laws involving other countries not to impose LWOP sentences against juveniles. The United States Constitution, the constitutions of the various states, and federal and state criminal codes are the only laws that matter.

Stimson [and Grossman's] work should be mandatory reading for anyone considering the propriety of LWOP punishments for young criminals. It doesn't matter whether [they're] right—it's enough that the other side is so wrong.

| "*I object to . . . the exaggerated hype (in terms of conveying the message that crime among young people is 'out of control') and in a few cases some downright untruths.*"

The Problem of Juvenile Crime Is Exaggerated by the Media

Randall G. Shelden

Using rare cases of horrific juvenile violence to exaggerate the problem of juvenile crime is unfair and misleading, argues University of Nevada criminal justice professor Randall G. Shelden in the following viewpoint. In fact, juvenile violent crime has declined significantly, Shelden maintains, and media accounts that cite the opinions of law enforcement officials give these views credibility when they are in fact just opinions. Indeed, he asserts, human perceptions are often inaccurate, and he concludes that since social conditions contribute to crime, policy makers should address poverty and other social problems rather than overreact based on unfounded portrayals of unfeeling, remorseless youth.

As you read, consider the following questions:

1. According to Shelden, what message did a series of articles appearing in the *Cape Cod Times* convey?

2. In the author's opinion, what was wrong with tables reporting crime statistics in the community of Barnstable?

3. According to Walter Lippmann, on what do people depend to keep themselves informed?

This past holiday season [2009] was spent on Cape Cod. Normally when I go away [for] the holidays I try to take a break from my routine and not pay much attention to news relating to crime and delinquency. However, I could not help but notice the first of a series of articles appearing in the *Cape Cod Times* shortly after I arrived. The title itself ("Younger and Twice as Violent") conveys a message to the reader that is not uncommon in this day of media hype and distortion. The message seems to be that crime is being committed by people younger than ever before and, even more frightening, the crimes are getting more violent with each passing day. After reading the series I just had to write a comment.

The appearance of this series is no coincidence, as it comes about one year after a particular brutal killing of 16-year-old Jordan Mendes by Mykel Mendes (Jordan's half-brother) and Kevin Ribeiro—both of whom were 13 at the time. The writers note that: "Local authorities say the case was extreme and unique in its circumstances for Cape Cod, but some experts argue that, nationally, teen murders are becoming more common."

Misleading Messages

I do not want to dismiss the horrible nature of the murder of this 16-year-old boy, nor the others who have been killed of late on Cape Cod—a few other cases are reported in the first part of this series (and it is interesting to note that each of these cases involved adults 18 or older). What I object to is the misleading nature of the points made in these articles, the exaggerated hype (in terms of conveying the message that crime among young people is "out of control") and in a few cases some downright untruths.

The untruths include a statement attributed to Northeastern University criminologist Jack Levin. Levin stated that "beginning in the mid-1980s, we observed a precipitous increase in murders and other serious crimes committed by 13-, 14-year-old boys and we've really almost had to redefine the lower limit of the violence-prone age group." This statement might cause the uninformed reader to conclude that the increase among this age group is still occurring today, which is patently not the case. According to the FBI's *Uniform Crime Reports* in 2008 only 3.3% of all arrests for violent crime involved those age 13 and 14. During the past ten years the arrests of those under 18 for violent crimes dropped by about 9%. The FBI report of 1999 noted that in the decade of the '90s violent crime by youths declined by 10%; in 1999 those age 13 and 14 accounted for just 3.7% of the violent crimes (not much different from 2008).

Misinterpreting the Evidence

Even in the 1980s the violent crime rate of juveniles was not nearly as bad as opinion makers made it out to be. Victimization studies support this. According to these studies the rate of violent crime by those under 18 was actually declining during the latter part of the decade. Actually, overall violence committed by youth in the 1980s was about the same as it was in the 1970s.

The authors of this article produce some very misleading tables, such as those pertaining to gunshot reports and overall crime statistics for Barnstable [a community of Cape Cod, Massachusetts]. In neither of these tables do they report what age group the figures pertain to. Do these crime statistics apply to all those under 18? Are these crimes reported to the police or arrests? Are these figures expressed as rates (per 100,000) or just actual numbers? What is the overall context of the gunshots? What proportion directly relates to crimes? How many turned out to be something other than guns (e.g., firecrackers, automobiles)?

Opinions, Not Facts

Contrary to the image conveyed by the title, the authors note that youth crime on the Cape has been going down (in a follow-up article the authors note that on the Cape "the number of juvenile delinquency complaints dropped by 36 percent between 2006 and 2008)," but then stated that "the severity of the crimes the police are seeing has reached a new peak." This statement was followed by the following quote from Barnstable police chief Paul MacDonald: "There aren't more weapons on the street, but it's more of a different mind-set by the individuals out there. They are certainly more willing to use them." Retired judge Richard Connon is quoted as follows: "There's a lot of younger defendants that come in here that show absolutely no remorse. They don't feel compassion for anybody that is suffering." The article brings out similar quotes from other public officials. Incidentally, most of the cases they are referring to are actually adults, not juveniles (one of many contradictions in this article).

These are merely opinions based upon individual perceptions, not facts (what proportion of kids coming to court are less remorseful?). It gives the reader the sense that "kids these days" are worse than ever, which is not true at all, as a recent study has found.

Changing Social Conditions

To their credit, the writers of this series note the context within which youth crime occurs, noting the large percentage living in poverty and other negative circumstances connected to the youth population. More than 100 years of research has reinforced the fact that these social conditions are largely responsible for crime (regardless of age). We must continue to work on the reduction of such conditions and provide as many alternatives for young offenders (and youth in general) as possible. I and many others have provided many examples of these alternatives. . . . As noted in a *Times* editorial, there are several ongoing successful efforts (e.g., Barnstable County Sheriff's Youth Academy and a diversion program operated within the district attorney's office) to address youth problems. These and others should be continued. It is a shame that money for prevention programs on the Cape has been reduced in recent years.

Almost 90 years ago Walter Lippmann wrote his classic work *Public Opinion* in which he argued that it is almost impossible for people to know very much through their own direct experience. Instead, Lippmann noted that we depend on "pictures in our heads," many delivered by the news media, to inform us about what is going on in the world. The news media has an important responsibility to be as accurate as possible. The media should rely more on factual evidence than perceptions, which often are a product of "confirmation bias"—where you tend to look for evidence that supports a preexisting bias and ignore contrary evidence.

> *"The fastest-growing criminal segment at both the state and federal levels [is] teenage girls."*

Adolescent Girls Are Becoming More Violent

Colleen O'Connor

In the following viewpoint, Denver Post *staff writer Colleen O'Connor asserts that a growing number of violent teen girls are entering the criminal justice system. Programs that address the needs of increasingly violent teen girls are therefore needed, she maintains. Because girls learn differently and have different motivations than boys, girls need unique programs, O'Connor claims. Physical, emotional, and sexual abuse is more common among girls than boys who enter the system, so programs that focus on how to build healthy relationships and trust with other women and girls should be a priority, she reasons. Programs that follow this model have shown some success but need further study, she concludes.*

As you read, consider the following questions:

1. What statistics does O'Connor cite to show that the spike in the number of teen girls in Colorado's juvenile justice system is also seen nationally?

2. According to the author, what percentage of incarcerated girls have experienced some form of abuse?

3. How do teen girls typically react when placed in all-girl intervention programs, according to Kimberly Bolding?

Guadalupe Herrera was an eighth grader at Skyview Middle School [in Colorado Springs, Colorado], a tough girl with attitude and a gang wardrobe, when she learned another girl was spreading rumors about her. One day, she walked by the girl, who pointed at her and began whispering.

"I said, 'If you've got something to say to me, say it to my face,'" said Guadalupe, who turned and walked away. "I wasn't even 5 feet away from her when she said, 'That psycho border-hopper.'"

"It was like a spit in the face," Guadalupe said. "I was born and raised here. I'm just as American as she is. My blood zoomed up. I started shaking."

Guadalupe's violent reaction, which ended with her arrest after pummeling her tormenter on a field outside the school, made her part of the fastest-growing criminal segment at both the state and federal levels: teenage girls.

"I hit her hard, with everything I had," Guadalupe said. "I was bombing on her."

A Growing Trend

In Colorado, while overall violent crime by girls has gone down, the number of assaults—such as Guadalupe's fistfight—has gone up about 5 percent a year since 2001, said Lisa Pasko, an assistant professor of sociology and criminology at the University of Denver.

Pasko has just completed a two-year study of violent middle school and high school girls in Colorado's juvenile justice system, funded by a grant from the Colorado Division of Criminal Justice, to find out how best to reduce the number of girls in the system and prevent recidivism. The report, scheduled to be presented to the state's juvenile justice delinquency prevention task force on Dec. 1 [2010] shows a spike in the number of girls in the system.

Between 2003 and 2006, the commitment rate for girls ages 12 to 17 increased 52 percent, while the detention rate increased 28 percent. Commitment is long-term incarceration, similar to prison, while detention is for shorter terms, like a county jail.

The trend is also seen nationally. Between 1999 and 2008, the number of girls arrested for common assaults rose 12.2 percent, while boys' arrests for the same crimes fell 5.8 percent.

"Some girls are saying that their lives are harder, and they're using violence as a strategy," said Pasko, who spent time with serious offenders. "There is more disconnection, more moms on parole or partnering with a guy who is not good or who is volatile."

A Tailor-Made Program Is Needed

In 1996, Colorado became one of the few states to create gender-specific guidelines for girls in the juvenile justice system, a comprehensive approach centered on female development and how girls learn.

A 2008 U.S. Department of Justice report cited as its most significant finding a "lack of reliable, accurate, and comprehensive information about good prevention and intervention programing for girls." The report went on to state that most of the programs "had not been evaluated to the degree that they could be considered 'effective.'"

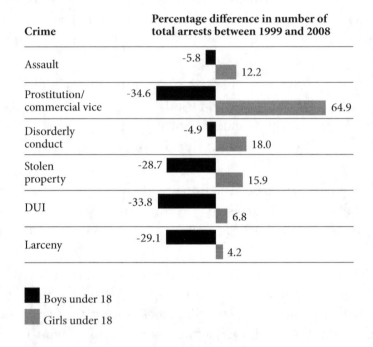

Rising Arrests Among Girls

During a period when overall crime has been falling in the United States, the number of girls arrested in several crime categories has been on the rise.

Crime	Percentage difference in number of total arrests between 1999 and 2008
Assault	Boys under 18: -5.8 / Girls under 18: 12.2
Prostitution/ commercial vice	Boys under 18: -34.6 / Girls under 18: 64.9
Disorderly conduct	Boys under 18: -4.9 / Girls under 18: 18.0
Stolen property	Boys under 18: -28.7 / Girls under 18: 15.9
DUI	Boys under 18: -33.8 / Girls under 18: 6.8
Larceny	Boys under 18: -29.1 / Girls under 18: 4.2

■ Boys under 18

■ Girls under 18

TAKEN FROM: Colleen O'Connor, "Fastest-Growing Segment of the Criminal Population? Teen Girls," *Denver Post*, October 20, 2010.

"The demand for these services is greater than ever," said Jeanne Smith, director of the Colorado Division of Criminal Justice. "As a state, we're trying to reduce recidivism . . . and a part of that is recognizing the demographics of offenders in the system, which has shown an increase in female offenders."

Girls learn differently from boys and are motivated by different things, so lowering the recidivism rate for girls depends on helping them in ways that work for them.

"Girls that come into the system have a lot of boundary issues, trust issues and problems in their relationships," Pasko said. "Many times, these unhealthy relationships are what is getting them into crime in the first place."

Teaching them how to have healthy relationships requires very small groups, which help build intimacy and trust and also target how girls think.

Girls in the juvenile justice system also have experienced childhood victimization at much higher rates than boys, according to [a] study . . . by Physicians for Human Rights.

Up to 92 percent of incarcerated girls have experienced some form of abuse—physical, emotional, sexual—before entering the system.

A Violent Past

For Guadalupe Herrera, domestic violence was a key factor. Her mother's boyfriend, who lived with them, started beating her when she was 4 years old.

"He was alcoholic," she said. "I was his beat-down toy. There wasn't a day when he didn't hit me."

He would throw her against a wall or "between his legs like a football," she said.

Eventually, her grandmother took Guadalupe and her older sister to live with her.

"My mom worked three jobs, and when she wasn't working, she was fighting with him," Guadalupe said.

It all stopped when she was about 10.

"He was beating my mom, and then he grabbed my little sister and threw her against the wall, and she was bleeding from her nose," Guadalupe said.

Guadalupe's mother called the police, and her boyfriend went to court, then received a five-year jail sentence. By then, Guadalupe was a fifth grader who had taught herself to be so tough that when boys tried to pick on her in school, they quickly learned that was a bad idea.

"This one boy tried to push me, so I pushed him back, and he fell to the floor and started crying," Guadalupe said. "When I did that, I felt this rush. I felt so good. They didn't pick on me anymore."

In eighth grade, arrested for assault, she ended up in teen court, where the judge sent her to an all-girl intervention program called InterCept Too in Colorado Springs.

She was furious.

"I told my mom, 'I'm not going to that stupid group. It's all girls, and I don't like girls. I will be going to juvenile hall, because I will knock somebody out.'"

Building on Breakthroughs

That's a typical reaction, said Kimberly Bolding, director of youth services at the Women's Resource Agency in Colorado Springs, who runs InterCept Too.

"Most girls who come here say, 'No, I can't do an all-girls group. I hate girls. All my friends are guys. Girls are haters,'" Bolding said.

The program focuses on teaching girls how to develop healthy relationships with girls and women, and how to channel their anger in positive ways.

But for more than half of the 10-week series of classes, Guadalupe hated them. She sat far in the back, away from the other girls. Mostly, she rolled her eyes and glared, speaking as little as possible.

"She had so much anger she couldn't see straight," Bolding said.

In the seventh session, when the topic was domestic abuse, she suddenly opened up and began to share her own experience. Bolding asked her how the abuse had affected her and how she coped with it.

"I said, 'I don't have coping skills. I don't even know what that is. I just suck it all in and keep it in until someone really makes me mad, and then I blow up on them,'" Guadalupe said.

After the 10-week session was over, Bolding kept working with Guadalupe in one-on-one counseling sessions and in meetings with her mother.

And though the Justice Department report states that "researchers are unsure how effective these programs are" because of a lack of evidence, Guadalupe is one of InterCept Too's success stories. Now 15, she hopes to eventually join the Air Force and attend college.

"I'm much happier now," she said. "Before, I would cuss you out and then hit you in the face. Now, I wouldn't even cuss you out. I'd just say what I had to say in a classier way."

| "There is no burgeoning national crisis of increasing serious violence among adolescent girls."

There Is No Evidence Showing a Rise in Violence Among Adolescent Girls

Margaret A. Zahn et al.

Despite shocking media stories and delinquency statistics, violent teen girls are not a growing trend, claims Margaret A. Zahn and her colleagues, who are part of the Girls Study Group, in the following viewpoint. Using arrest statistics, self-report data, and victimization surveys, the authors conclude that the incidence of teen girl violence has not changed much since the late 1980s. Thus, the authors argue, enforcement policies, not changing female behavior, are responsible for increasing arrest numbers. Moreover, the group suggests, the context of violence is different for girls than boys. To prevent violence among teen girls, they reason, research is needed to understand under what circumstances girls respond violently. The Girls Study Group is a program of the Office of Juvenile Justice and Delinquency Prevention, which is part of the US Department of Justice.

Margaret A. Zahn et al., *Girls Study Group: Understanding and Responding to Girls' Delinquency*, May 2008. www.ncjrs.gov. Office of Juvenile Justice and Delinquency Prevention.

As you read, consider the following questions:

1. According to the authors, what agency is the primary source of official data on delinquency?

2. What is the main benefit of self-report data, in the authors' view?

3. In the authors' opinion, why do girls fight with peers?

In June 2005, *Newsweek* ran a story titled "Bad Girls Go Wild," which described "the significant rise in violent behavior among girls" as a "burgeoning national crisis"—a depiction that echoes other recent media accounts. This [viewpoint] assesses the accuracy of these assertions using the best available data. Drawing on information from official arrest sources, nationally based self-report and victimization surveys, and studies reported in the social science literature, the [viewpoint] examines the involvement of girls in violent activity (including whether such activity has increased relative to the increase for boys) and the contexts in which girls engage in violent behavior.

Interpreting Arrest Statistics

One of the most consistent and robust findings in criminology is that, for nearly every offense, females engage in much less crime and juvenile delinquency than males. In recent years, however, the extent and character of this gender difference in offending are increasingly being called into question by statistics and media reports suggesting the increasing involvement of girls in the juvenile and criminal justice systems. During the past two-and-a-half decades, official statistics suggest that female delinquency has undergone substantial changes compared with male delinquency. Between 1980 and 2005, arrests of girls increased nationwide, while arrests of boys decreased. These arrest trends, along with high-profile cases of female delinquency, have become the main support for media headlines.

45

However, because arrest counts are a product of both delinquent behavior and official responses to it, researchers and policy makers face a dilemma about how to interpret the arrest statistics. Do the increases in arrests indicate real changes in girls' behaviors, or are the increases a product of recent changes in public sentiment and enforcement policies that have elevated the visibility and reporting of girls' delinquency and violence? This [viewpoint] attempts to answer this question.

The Data Sources

This [viewpoint] relies on three data sources—official arrest data, self-report data, and victimization data—to examine trends in girls' violence from 1980 through 2005. Each source has strengths and weaknesses and provides a somewhat different picture of crime.

Official sources of data on delinquency include information collected and disseminated by local agencies such as police, as well as state and national organizations that disseminate information collected at the local level. The primary source of official data on delinquency comes from the Federal Bureau of Investigation's (FBI's) *Uniform Crime Reports* (UCR), published annually. Each UCR reflects thousands of local police reports on crimes known to police and on arrests, from which the FBI compiles statistics on the type of crime (roughly 30 broad categories), the location of the arrest (urban, suburban, or rural), and the demographic characteristics of the offender (e.g., age, gender).

Self-report surveys on juvenile crime and its correlates are another major source of information. In addition to the detailed information on respondent characteristics, the main benefit of self-report data is the information obtained on crimes that were committed by youth but not known to the police. Most self-report delinquency surveys are cross-sectional (i.e., cover only one point in time) and localized (i.e., limited to a particular community or region). Among the surveys that provide longitudinal or trend data on youth delinquency for the nation as a whole, the authors use Monitoring the Future (MTF). MTF is an ongoing study of the behaviors, attitudes, and values of American secondary school students. Each year, a total of approximately 50,000 8th-, 10th-, and 12th-grade students are surveyed (12th graders since 1975, and 8th and 10th graders since 1991).

Victimization surveys provide a third important source of information on delinquent behavior. These types of data provide a different perspective. Whereas information on self-reported delinquent activity is collected from the offender, the source of information for victimization surveys is the victim of criminal activity. The Census Bureau has conducted the National Crime Victimization Survey (NCVS) for the Bureau of Justice Statistics annually since 1973. Each year, NCVS interviews individuals age 12 and older in a nationally representative sample of approximately 50,000 households. Victims of various types of crimes (including violent and property crimes) report detailed characteristics of criminal events, including time and location, level of physical and property damage, and—in the case of violent crime—the perceived characteristics (e.g., age, gender, race) of the offender(s)....

The Trends

Available evidence based on arrest, victimization, and self-report data suggests that although girls are currently arrested more for simple assaults than previously, the actual incidence of their being seriously violent has not changed much over the last two decades. This suggests that increases in arrests may be attributable more to changes in enforcement policies than to changes in girls' behavior. Juvenile female involvement in violence has not increased relative to juvenile male violence. There is no burgeoning national crisis of increasing serious violence among adolescent girls.

Type of Victim in Aggravated and Simple Assaults by Boys and Girls

| | Simple Assault | | Aggravated Assault | |
Type of Victim	Boys	Girls	Boys	Girls
Juvenile family	5%	5%	4%	7%
Juvenile acquaintance	54	49	45	40
Juvenile stranger	5	3	6	2
Adult family	17	23	12	21
Adult acquaintance	16	17	21	24
Adult stranger	4	3	12	6

TAKEN FROM: Girls Study Group (OJJDP), *Violence by Teenage Girls: Trends and Context*, May 2008.

Although more information is needed, current literature suggests that girls' violence occurs in the following situations, for the following reasons:

- Peer violence. Girls fight with peers to gain status, to defend their sexual reputation, and in self-defense against sexual harassment.

- Family violence. Girls fight more frequently at home with parents than do boys, who engage more frequently in violence outside the household. Girls' violence against parents is multidimensional: for some, it represents striking back against what they view as an overly controlling structure; for others, it is a defense against or an expression of anger stemming from being sexually and or physically abused by members of the household.

- Violence within schools. When girls fight in schools, they may do so as a result of teacher labeling, in self-defense, or out of a general sense of hopelessness.

- Violence within disadvantaged neighborhoods. Girls in disadvantaged neighborhoods are more likely to perpetrate violence against others because of the increased risk of victimization (and the resulting violent self-defense against that victimization), parental inability to counteract negative community influences, and lack of opportunities for success.

- Girls in gangs. Survey research has shown a number of factors associated with girls' involvement in gangs (e.g., attitudes toward school, peers, delinquency, drug use, and early sexual activity); qualitative research points to the role of disadvantaged neighborhoods and families with multiple problems (violence, drug and alcohol abuse, neglect). Girls associated with primarily male gangs exhibit more violence than those in all-female gangs. Girls in gangs are more violent than other girls but less violent than boys in gangs.

What We Need to Know

Available evidence strongly suggests that girls are, over time, being arrested more frequently for simple assaults, despite evidence from longitudinal self-report and victimization surveys that they are not actually more violent. The reasons for increasing arrests, however, are not well established. Studies of police and court practices—particularly with regard to girls—are sorely needed. Evaluations of domestic violence laws and zero-tolerance school policies and enforcement practices are also crucial.

It is also important to develop a better understanding of the consequences for girls of increased involvement in the juvenile justice system. Longitudinal studies of girls who are arrested for assaultive behavior would help us better understand the pathways to and consequences of arrests for violent behavior among girls.

Although there does not appear to be a large increase in physical violence committed by girls, some girls do engage in violent behavior, and it is important to understand the context in which such violence occurs and how these situations differ for girls and boys. Although peers and family members are the most common targets of violence by girls, not all family or peer conflicts result in physical assault. Understanding which ones do, and why, remains vital for both prevention and intervention efforts.

> *"The 14-year gang prevalence trend . . . demonstrates that gang activity remains a widespread problem across the United States."*

Youth Gangs Are a Serious Problem

James C. Howell et al.

Although crime has declined dramatically nationwide, youth gang violence continues to be a serious problem, claims James C. Howell, and his colleagues Arlen Egley Jr., George E. Tita, and Elizabeth Griffiths, in the following viewpoint. In Los Angeles and Chicago between 1996 and 2009, for example, as many as 40 percent of homicides were gang related, the authors assert. To develop effective policies to address gang violence, they argue, policy makers must assess the overall role gangs play in youth violence. Indeed, the authors maintain, states significantly impacted by gang homicides should monitor the problem in the same way they monitor disease threats. Howell and Egley conduct research for the National Gang Center; Tita is a criminology professor at the University of California, Irvine; and Griffiths is a sociology professor at Emory University.

James C. Howell et al., "U.S. Gang Problem Trends and Seriousness, 1996–2009," *National Gang Center Bulletin*, no. 6, May 2011, pp. 1–3, 6, 10, 13–14. Copyright © 2011 by Office of Juvenile Justice and Delinquency Prevention. All rights reserved. Reproduced by permission.

As you read, consider the following questions:

1. According to the authors, where did serious gangs first emerge and when?

2. What percentage of the jurisdictions studied by the National Youth Gang Survey experienced gang problems in 2009?

3. According to the authors, what percentage of the homicides in Los Angeles were gang related in 2009?

Street gangs did not develop uniformly across the United States. Serious gangs first emerged on the East Coast in the 1820s, led by New York City (Howell and Moore, 2010). A half century would pass before gangs emerged in the Midwestern (Chicago) area and Western (Los Angeles) regions, which would see significant gang development a full century later than New York City. The South would not experience significant gang problems for almost another half century, starting in the 1960s. . . .

Tracking the Gang Problem

The National Gang Center (NGC)[1] has tracked the distribution and level of the gang problem in the United States since its first nationally representative National Youth Gang Survey (NYGS), in 1996. The NYGS is the first gang survey in any country that annually contacts a nationally representative sample of authoritative respondents in their respective jurisdictions regarding the prevalence and characteristics of gang activity using the same methodology each year. With the accumulation of 14 years of data, this report provides a long-term view of data generated in the NYGS, covering the time period from 1996 to 2009.[2]

1. The National Gang Center was formerly called the National Youth Gang Center.
2. For previous NGS publications covering relatively short time segments, see Egley Howell, and Major (2004, 2006); Howell (2006); Howell and Egley (2005); Howell and Gleason (1999); Howell, Egley, and Gleason (2002); and Howell, Moore, and Egley (2002).

The 14-year gang prevalence trend . . . demonstrates that gang activity remains a widespread problem across the United States. By 2009, prevalence rates were significantly elevated compared with recorded lows in 2000 and 2001. Approximately one-third of the jurisdictions in the NYGS study population experienced gang problems in 2009, compared with under one-quarter in 2002, an increase of more than 20 percent in the estimated number of gang-problem jurisdictions between 2002 and 2009. . . .

Larger cities consistently exhibit the highest prevalence rates of gang activity among the four groups, followed by, in order, suburban counties, smaller cities, and rural counties.[3] The rates of reported gang activity in suburban counties are closest to the rates for larger cities because of the relatively large populations in suburban counties (i.e., a high capacity to sustain gang activity, Egley et al., 2006), the shifting of previous inner-city slums and ghettos to ring-city or suburban areas (Miller, 2001), and the growing popularity of gang culture in these areas (Miller, 2001). . . .

Serious Gang-Problem Trends

Cities can be grouped in terms of their distinctively patterned gang-problem histories. With this in mind, the next step is to assess the relative seriousness of gang activity among cities. For the purposes of this analysis, homicide is considered to be a primary indicator of serious gang activity.

While homicides notably characterize serious gang-problem cities more than any other factor, it is important to note that gang homicides are heavily concentrated geographically in the United States. Most cities have no gang homicides,

3. The upturn in suburban counties from 2008 to 2009 is the result of a group of agencies newly reporting gang problems in their jurisdictions to the NYGS. However, based on the initial data submitted by these agencies, the gang problem appears relatively small in size (e.g., fewer than 20 gang members) and magnitude (all of the agencies with the exception of one reported zero gang homicides) in these areas.

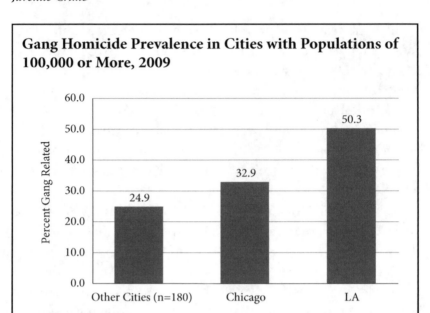

Gang Homicide Prevalence in Cities with Populations of 100,000 or More, 2009

TAKEN FROM: James C. Howell et al., "U.S. Gang Problem Trends and Seriousness, 1996–2009," *National Gang Center Bulletin*, May 2011.

and those that do usually report very few of them from year to year (Egley et al., 2006). Rather, it is in a subset of very large cities where the overwhelming majority of them occur. . . .

We explore some dimensions of the current concentration of high homicide levels in very large U.S. cities. Chart 1 shows the total percent of homicides that were gang related among cities with populations of 100,000 or more in 2009 (for which homicide data were reported). Separate figures are presented for Chicago and Los Angeles because of their historically high numbers of gang homicides. Overall, approximately one-quarter of all homicides in these cities were gang related. By comparison, one-half of the homicides in Los Angeles and one-third of the homicides in Chicago were gang related in 2009. . . .

The Implications

Gang activity and its associated violence remains an important and significant component of the U.S. crime problem. While it has been reasonably assumed that gang-related violence would follow the overall dramatic declines in violent crime nationally, analyses provided in this report find overwhelming evidence to the contrary—that is, gang-violence rates have continued at exceptional levels over the past decade *despite* the remarkable overall crime drop. Gang violence that is rather commonplace in very large cities seems largely unaffected by, if not independent from, other crime trends—with the possible exceptions of drug trafficking and firearm availability (Block and Block, 1993; Block et al., 1996; Howell, 1999; Tita and Cohen, 2004; Tita and Griffiths, 2005; Tita and Ridgeway, 2007).

This study has shown that while fluctuations in the prevalence of gang activity are certainly evident since the mid-1990s to the present, much of this instability has occurred outside the largest U.S. cities where gang activity has remained concentrated and prevalence rates have remained nearly constant. In addition, and perhaps more important, the seriousness of gang problems in these cities has not changed appreciably in this period. Two distinct groups of very large cities (with populations greater than 100,000 persons), together making up 70 percent of all large cities, consistently reported that between 20 and 40 percent of their homicides were gang related from 1996 to 2009; and only *one group*, composed of less than one-quarter of the cities, exhibited very few to no gang homicides in the study period. Moreover, reported gang-related homicides in these cities increased 7 percent from 2005 to 2009 (Egley and Howell, forthcoming).

Developing a strategic plan for intervening in gang homicides is complicated by gang dynamics. [According to George E. Tita and A. Abrahamse,] "Even labeling something as a 'gang' homicide masks important aspects that need to be understood before enacting policy; for example, whether the homicide was motivated by gang rivalry, or the protection of drug markets, or was merely an argument that involved young males who happened to be gang members" (Tita and Abrahamse, 2010, p. 29). These situations underscore the importance of making a careful assessment of overall youth violence and the gang component before developing a strategic plan (Tita, Riley, and Ridgeway, 2003). A user-friendly protocol is available that communities themselves can follow in conducting a community-wide assessment (Office of Juvenile Justice and Delinquency Prevention, 2009). Analysis of the specific circumstances surrounding gang homicides also greatly increases the likelihood of successful interventions (Braga, 2004). . . .

In most jurisdictions, improvements are needed in the targeting of gang violence. To aid statewide initiatives, Tita and Abrahamse (2010) recommended that California implement a gang homicide surveillance system, designed much like systems used by the public health community to monitor disease threats. The proposed system would provide an early warning of a rise in homicide victimization within particular communities, much like the public health model. In addition, Tita and Abrahamse suggest that such a homicide surveillance system needs to work fast enough to provide a warning within a few months of gang homicide onset. "It also needs to be fine grained with respect to geography and demography" (p. 29). However, reporting should not be delayed until a homicide is "solved," they argue, because early intervention opportunities could be lost. In addition, such a system should capture and publish essential diagnostic information (including age, race, sex, circumstance, and census tract) about suspected homicide victims within a month of the event, which "would provide an important tool for detecting and reacting to upswings in violence in the state" (p. 29). This is an excellent recommendation for other states and cities with gang-related homicides.

"All of the available evidence indicates that gang members play a relatively small role in the crime problem."

The Problem of Youth Gangs Is Exaggerated

Judith Greene and Kevin Pranis

The commonly held belief that youth gangs are well-organized bands of criminals responsible for much of violent crime is mostly myth, maintain Judith Greene and Kevin Pranis in the following viewpoint. In fact, they argue, defining homicides by motive significantly reduces gang homicide statistics. Indeed, Greene and Pranis claim, of the gang homicides that were studied, half served personal rather than gang interests. While youth gang violence is a serious problem, overstating gang crime figures and labeling all gang members criminals leads to ineffective public policies. Greene and Pranis are criminal justice policy analysts writing for the Justice Policy Institute, which opposes society's reliance on incarceration.

Judith Greene and Kevin Pranis, "Chapter 6: Public Enemy #1? Gang Crime Myths and Realities," *Gang Wars: The Failure of Enforcement Tactics and the Need for Effective Public Safety Strategies*, July 2007, pp. 51–53, 61–62. Copyright © 2007 by Justice Policy Institute. All rights reserved. Reproduced by permission.

As you read, consider the following questions:

1. In the opinion of Greene and Pranis, what did ethnographic and survey research show about how gang members spend their time?

2. According to the authors, what is the methodological weakness of youth self-reports?

3. What explanations do the authors give for why law enforcement and media reports consistently overestimate the role of gangs in crime and violence?

Gangs can be understood in many ways. John Hagedorn and Sudhir Venkatesh describe gangs as replacements for mainstream institutions (the state, the family) that find themselves in crisis. Others such as Luis Barrios and David Brotherton argue that gangs take on aspects of social movements. Finally, many have observed that gangs proliferate and operate within the realm of youth culture, citing among other examples the role of the film *Colors* in the dissemination of Los Angeles gang culture.

Myths About Gangs and Crime

But the dominant public discourse treats gangs as a particularly virulent subset of the crime problem. James Short and Lorine Hughes argue that this tendency has affected gang studies, which largely *"regard gangs as a fractal of crime."* The tendency to equate gangs with the most spectacular forms of crime has also generated a set of public myths about the relationship between gangs and crime. These myths hold that:

- Most or all gang members are hardened criminals.

- Gang members spend most of their time planning or committing crimes.

- Gang members are responsible for the bulk of violent crime.

- Gangs largely organize and direct the criminal activity of their members.

There may be a handful of gangs and gang members who meet this description. Researchers who study gangs generally find, however, that most "gang crime" is not well planned or centrally directed, but is instead committed by individual members or small groups on an ad hoc basis.

Ethnographic and survey research have fairly consistently shown that:

- The seriousness and extent of criminal involvement varies greatly among gang members.

- Gang members who engage in crime nonetheless spend most of their time in noncriminal pursuits.

- Gang members account for a small share of all crime (including violent crime), even within communities and neighborhoods where there are gang problems.

- Much of the crime committed by gang members is self-initiated and is meant to serve personal rather than gang interests.

What Is a Gang Crime?

Law enforcement officials generally employ one of two definitions of gang crime for the purposes of tracking and measuring the problem. The first counts all crimes committed by individuals who are believed to be gang members as *gang related*, regardless of the nature of the offense or the circumstances surrounding it. The second and more restrictive definition includes only *gang-motivated* crimes that are believed to have been committed for the benefit of the gang or as part of a gang function.

Cheryl Maxson and Malcolm Klein examined police data in South Central Los Angeles and found that use of a motive-based definition generated half as many gang homicides as a member-based definition. In other words, half of the homicides committed by gang members were not committed for the gang or as part of gang activity.

Gang-motivated crimes can be further divided into two categories: *self-directed* crimes that are initiated and organized by individuals or small groups of rank-and-file gang members, and *gang-directed* crimes commissioned or orchestrated by gang leaders or the gang as a whole. Finally, gang-motivated crimes can be understood in terms of *instrumental* actions that are intended to advance the material interests of the gang or its leaders, and *expressive* actions that show gang pride and demonstrate that the group is more fearless than its rivals by defending turf, avenging past injuries, and so on.

Defining Four Cases

Consider the following four cases:

1. A gang member gets in a fight with another man who makes a pass at his girlfriend at a party.

2. A gang member assaults a young man affiliated with a rival gang who has ventured onto territory claimed by the subject's gang.

3. A gang member is asked by older gang members to go on a "mission" into enemy territory to find and attack rival gang members.

4. A gang member is asked by gang leaders to punish a witness who testified against another member.

All four cases would fall under the member-based definition of gang crime, but the first would not meet the motive-based definition because the fight had nothing to do with the gang. The third and fourth cases could be considered gang-directed incidents, but not the second, which was initiated spontaneously by the individual in question.

The fourth case could represent an instrumental effort to advance gang members' material interests by deterring witnesses from testifying against the gang. The third case, by contrast, depicts what is probably an expressive use of gang violence that is more likely to harm than to help gang members' material interests by generating further violence and drawing unwanted attention from law enforcement.

Tales of sophisticated criminal conspiracies and calculated use of violence dominate the public discussion of gang crime. But gang-directed, instrumental activities are the exception, not the rule. Descriptions of gang activity drawn from ethnography and survey research provide little support for the view that gangs are a form of organized crime.

As a general rule, gang members do not spend hours carefully planning out robberies and burglaries with their fellows. They do not turn drug revenues over to the gang to finance its activities, but instead spend their money on clothes and fast food, as many other teenagers do. And most do not wait for permission from higher-ups to attack members of a rival group. Many gang youth engage in violence, but it is overwhelmingly expressive in nature and often initiated by rank-and-file members—at times *against* the wishes of gang leaders who seek to keep a lid on conflicts. Drug sales are also common among gang members, but the activity generally ranges from a completely disorganized pursuit of individuals to loosely organized cooperative endeavors.

The Disorganized Nature of Gang Crime

The disorganized character of most gang crime does not reduce its significance. Nor can we ignore the moments when the wrong set of circumstances generates the kind of gang threat that we most fear. Short recounts the efforts of Richard Brymmer to locate the large youth gangs that had been described to him by police and neighborhood residents. After encountering only small groupings of eight to ten youth (*palomillas*) for two years, Brymmer witnessed the sudden transformation of the *palomillas* into a "wall of young males" in response to a threat from a rival gang. The transformation of the *palomillas* into a gang was a rare occurrence, but one with potentially lethal consequences.

But the disorganized character of gang crime does raise the question of whether a gang is best understood as an organization with defined leadership, goals, and means to achieve those goals, or as an activity that orients youth toward crime and conflict with other gang members. Understanding the disorganized character of gang crime also makes it possible to consider the degree to which getting rid of gang leaders, or even the gang itself, is likely to affect the incidence of crime and violence.

Measuring Gang Crime and Delinquency

There are three methods for measuring gang crime and delinquency:

- self-reports of delinquent activity by youth who identify themselves as gang members;

- self-reports of victimization by people who believe that their attacker was a gang member; and

- police reports of crimes committed by known or suspected gang members (typically generated at arrest).

Each type of data has methodological weaknesses. Youth self-reports may inflate or minimize delinquent behaviors if the respondents seek to exaggerate or conceal their involvement in them. Most surveys of youth gang activity target specific locations or segments of the youth population, making it difficult to derive general conclusions about the larger youth gang population. Finally, many of the relevant surveys include only youth under the age of 18 and ignore a young adult gang population that is of great interest to law enforcement, although the Denver and Rochester youth surveys have continued to collect information from participants into their adult years.

The respondents in the National Crime Victimization Survey (NCVS) report victimization by people whom they believe to be gang members, a belief that could be inaccurate or influenced by outside factors such as media reports of gang activity. Further, NCVS data are reported only at the national level and cannot be used to track regional or local trends.

No Agreed-Upon Definition

Law enforcement gang crime numbers include only crimes that are reported to police and identified by the police as gang related or gang motivated. There is no agreed-upon definition of a gang or a gang crime, much less a uniform system for tracking and reporting it. Finally, the capacity and criteria for measuring gang crime vary greatly between law enforcement agencies and can shift from year to year as priorities change. A number of gang researchers have collaborated with police to improve data collection or used police records to conduct their own analyses of crime data, but these efforts are few and far between.

Deborah Lamm Weisel and Tara O'Connor Shelley warn that "while it is tempting to use law enforcement data about gangs and gang-related offenses to make comparisons between—or even within—jurisdictions, gang-related data are exceptionally unreliable for this purpose." Law enforcement data provide no more than a blurry snapshot of the scale of gang crime in a particular jurisdiction in a particular year. Nonetheless, law enforcement gang crime reports are frequently cited because they are often the only figures that can be compared to overall crime reports at the local level.

With the exception of law enforcement agencies that employ the less common motive-based definition, all three measures track crimes committed by gang members that may or may not be gang motivated. The use of a broad membership-based definition overstates the contribution of gangs to the crime problem, since some members would engage in criminal activity whether or not they were affiliated with a gang. . . .

Perception and Reality

All of the available evidence indicates that gang members play a relatively small role in the crime problem despite their propensity toward criminal activity. Gang members appear to be responsible for fewer than one in four drug sales; fewer than one in 10 homicides; fewer than one in 16 violent offenses; and fewer than one in 20 index crimes. Gangs themselves play an even smaller role, since much of the crime committed by gang members is self-directed and not committed for the gang's benefit. The question, then, is why the problem of gang crime is so commonly overstated by law enforcement and media reports.

There are several possible explanations for why law enforcement and media reports consistently overestimate the role of gangs and gang members in crime and violence. First, gang members often make themselves highly visible, while others who commit crimes try to keep a lower profile in order to avoid arrest. Graffiti, colors, hand signs, and dramatic rivalries ensure that gang activity will be more memorable and more newsworthy than the less spectacular offenses that drive crime statistics.

Fueling Gang Crime Myths

Second, law enforcement and media depictions of gangs fuel gang crime myths by equating all gang activity with criminal activity and by tarring all gangs and members with the worst crimes committed by any gang member. Klein succinctly illustrates the tendency of law enforcement agencies to cram all drug crime in a gang box when he quotes the deputy chief of a large police department on the subject of crack sales:

> Look, this narcotics stuff is all a matter of gangs and conspiracy. To me, a gang is any two or more guys working on crime together. In a drug sale, you got at least the seller and the distributor involved. Now that means it's a conspiracy. And there's two guys, right. So all these crack sales are gang crimes. . . . Two or more guys conspiring to make crack sales means it's a gang affair . . . that's how we define gang around here.

Law enforcement and media accounts also tend to attribute to the gang any crime for which an alleged gang member stands convicted, charged, or even suspected. This practice implies that every member of a gang has committed, or is at least capable of committing, a laundry list of heinous offenses. Some agencies such as North Carolina's State Bureau of Investigation (SBI) go even further by lumping together the alleged activities of many gangs. The gangs of Charlotte/Mecklenburg County, for example, are said to engage in:

> homicides, threats against law enforcement, firearm possession, drug possession, assaults, fighting, kidnapping, carjacking, armed robbery, home invasions, vandalism (graffiti), auto theft, breaking into vehicles, restaurant robberies, gun trafficking, extortion, prostitution and gambling.

The list of alleged gang activities creates the impression that every Charlotte gang member is a sociopath with a long criminal record, or, at a minimum, that every gang contains murderers, drug traffickers, carjackers, armed robbers, and their ilk. A quick review of the national gang data dispels any such idea.

The typical gang is not an army of killers or even potential killers. It is a group of youth and young adults who are alienated from mainstream society and caught up in a mythical world of excitement and danger. The damage that these young people do to themselves, to each other, and to more than a few bystanders is very real. But as Klein and many other researchers have observed, most gang members are more talk than action. A more realistic assessment of the gang contribution to the crime problem is needed if policy makers are to avoid playing into the gang myth by inflating the dangers to public safety posed by gangs.

Periodical and Internet Sources Bibliography

The following articles have been selected to supplement the diverse views presented in this chapter.

Thomas J. Billitteri	"Youth Violence," *CQ Researcher*, March 5, 2010.
Erik Eckholm	"Murders by Black Teenagers Rise This Decade, Bucking a Trend," *New York Times*, December 29, 2008.
Arlen Egley Jr. and James C. Howell	"Highlights of the 2009 National Youth Gang Survey," *Juvenile Justice Fact Sheet*, June 2011.
James Alan Fox and Marc L. Swatt	"The Recent Surge in Homicides Involving Young Black Males and Guns: Time to Reinvest in Prevention and Crime Control," Northeastern University, December 2008.
Sandra Graham	"What Educators Need to Know About Bullying Behaviors," *Phi Delta Kappan*, September 2010.
Kristin Gray	"African American Youth Face Growing Threat from Peers," New American Media, October 7, 2009. http://news.newamericamedia.org.
Ken MacQueen	"How to Fight the Gangs: Gang-Related Crime Is Rising, Overwhelming the Authorities. But Something Can Be Done," *Maclean's*, March 12, 2009.
Kelly Richards	"What Makes Juvenile Offenders Different from Adult Offenders?," *Trends & Issues in Crime and Criminal Justice*, February 2011.
Victor Rivero and Ken Trump	"The Politicization of Bullying," *District Administration*, January 2011.

OPPOSING
VIEWPOINTS®
SERIES

CHAPTER 2

What Are the Causes of Juvenile Crime and Violence?

Chapter Preface

Since the root of a problem often determines prevention policies, the debate over causes can be quite contentious. In the juvenile crime debate, physicians and social scientists, as well as legal and policy analysts, have explored a wide variety of causes. One of the most hotly debated public policies concerns the disproportionate number of minority youths in the juvenile justice system. Most agree that disproportionate minority contact (DMC) is a serious problem. Indeed, a 2007 report prepared by the National Council on Crime and Delinquency reveals that while making up only 16 percent of youth in the general population, African Americans, for example, make up 28 percent of youth arrested, 34 percent of youth processed by juvenile courts, 38 percent of youth in residential placement, and 58 percent of youth admitted to state adult prison. The report's authors conclude, "While 'Equal Justice Under the Law' is the foundation of our legal system . . . the juvenile justice system is anything but equal for all. Throughout the system, youth of color—especially African American youth—receive different and harsher treatment for similar offenses."[1] The council calls for an effort to identify the causes of this differentiated treatment and policies to address the problem.

Some analysts argue, however, that determining causes based on juvenile justice statistics can be challenging. According to Charles Puzzanchera and Ben Adams of the Justice Department's National Center for Juvenile Justice, several factors could lead to DMC at arrest. "Minority youth may commit delinquencies at a greater rate than white youth. . . . It may also be that even when minority and white youth commit crimes at similar rates, the crimes of minority youth are

---

1. National Council on Crime and Delinquency, *And Justice for Some: Differential Treatment of Youth of Color in the Justice System*, January 2007.

more likely to be reported to law enforcement. . . . Or it could be that . . . law enforcement is more likely to arrest minority youth,"[2] they maintain. Nevertheless, Puzzanchera and Adams argue, statistics alone do not prove that the racial disparity is due to racial bias. Jeffrey Butts, executive director of the Criminal Justice Research and Evaluation Center at the John Jay College of Criminal Justice, agrees, adding that high arrest rates in minority neighborhoods may be due to the reality that "that's where the police are."[3] Butts also points out that harsh realities in impoverished urban neighborhoods may contribute to minority overrepresentation. Gangs often take advantage of vulnerable teens, and jobs are often hard to come by. "It would be nice if we could eliminate economic and housing disparities and then see what racial disparities are left over," Butts claims, "but we can't."[4]

Juvenile justice reform advocates agree that the problem is complex but point to recent policies that they assert lead to the persistence of DMC despite nationwide efforts to reduce the problem. For example, the Sentencing Project, a national advocacy organization that promotes reforms in sentencing law and alternatives to incarceration, argues that criminalizing school infractions through the implementation of harsh zero-tolerance policies has had an especially negative impact on minorities. Indeed, the police presence is more significant in urban low-income school districts that include large numbers of minorities. While school officials used to handle altercations at schools, the police are now called in and what was once a scuffle has become an assault, the project maintains. Once minorities have contact with the criminal justice system, they are more likely to have future contact. "Contact with the justice system reduces options for education, housing, and

2. Charles Puzzanchera and Ben Adams, *An Interpretation of the National DMC Relative Rate Indices for Juvenile Justice System Processing in 2008*, National Center for Juvenile Justice, May 2011.
3. Thomas J. Billitteri, "Youth Violence," *CQ Researcher*, March 5, 2010.
4. *Ibid.*

employment, and also weakens the stability of communities of color and results in a deepening of the divide between whites and nonwhites,"[5] the project reasons.

Whether analysts can identify causes, and in turn which policies will best address the complex problem of DMC, remains to be seen. The authors in the following chapter explore other causes of juvenile crime and violence, further advancing the debate over what policies will address the problem.

5. The Sentencing Project, "Disproportionate Minority Contact," Fact Sheet, May 2010.

> "A review of almost 600 studies shows
> three main results of media violence:
> aggression, desensitization, and fear."

Media Violence Can Lead to Juvenile Violence

Carmela Lomonaco, Tia Kim, and Lori Ottaviano

For decades researchers have found a correlation between media violence and aggression, claims Carmela Lomonaco, Tia Kim, and Lori Ottaviano in the following viewpoint. Some have questioned the validity of such correlations, suggesting that studies conducted in laboratory settings cannot be applied to the real world. However, in a recent real-world study, forty-two percent of fourteen-year-old males who viewed television more than three hours a day were involved in violent incidents, the authors maintain. Because TV, movies, video games, and the Internet expose children to numerous acts of violence, parents should limit access to these media outlets, the authors conclude. Lomonaco conducts research for Sociometrics Corporation; Kim is a profes-

sor of Human Development and Family Studies at Perm State National Research University; and Ottaviano is a graduate student at the University of California, Riverside.

As you read, consider the following questions:

1. In the opinion of Lomonaco, Kim, and Ottaviano, what percentage of violent behavior reports correlate with violent Internet websites?
2. What type of changes in behavior do critics claim violent media studies focused on, according to the authors?
3. What was the purpose of the Telecommunications Act of 1996?

Children and adolescents have access to and consume a variety of different media forms, including television, the Internet, music and music videos, film and video games, many of which contain high levels of violent content. The concern (and the controversy) lies in whether violent content in media affects a young person's beliefs and behaviors, and more specifically, if frequent exposure contributes to increased aggression and even violence in young people.

Much of the research on the relationship between media exposure and aggression supports such a connection. Although critics have challenged the validity of these findings, suggesting that the studies focused only on short-term effects and were conducted in controlled laboratory settings, one study suggests that exposure to violent media in home environments has long-term implications.

Promising strategies for reducing exposure to media violence are available and include limit setting by parents/guardians, technological innovations such as the V-chip (which blocks inappropriate shows or content from being viewed by children), and media literacy training.

The Scope of the Problem

Most American homes (99%) have a television set, and [according to Eugene V. Beresin] "over half of all children have a television set in their bedrooms." After sleeping, watching television is the most frequent activity of children. The average child spends 28 hours a week watching television. By the time the average child is 18 years old, he or she will have witnessed 200,000 acts of violence, including 16,000 murders. Up to 20 acts of violence per hour occur in children's programming.

Movies, music videos, video games, and the Internet also contain high levels of violent content correlated with youth violence. Internet websites showing violence (killing, shooting, fighting, etc.) correlate with a 50% increase in reports of seriously violent behavior. Violence on the Internet is also possibly the most damaging and in need of more research. In 2003, about 12.5% of roughly 22 million adolescents (10–14 years old) saw 40 of the most violent movies. One recent study showed a physiological connection with desensitization to violent video games. There is little research on the effects of music videos and behavior, but there is limited information on rap videos and their effect on aggressive attitudes.

The Media as a Risk Factor

The relationship between exposure to violent media and aggression has been researched extensively over the past 30 years. Different types of studies have confirmed a correlation. A review of almost 600 studies shows three main results of media violence: aggression, desensitization, and fear. Exposure to media violence also has been correlated with changes in youth attitudes about the use of violence in interpersonal relationships. While the evidence may be compelling, translation of these findings to the "real" world has been problematic. Findings are criticized on the grounds that most studies were conducted under controlled laboratory conditions and focused on short-term changes in behavior. It is unclear whether violent

The Fox Guarding the Henhouse

Though broadcasters claim that they care about the concerns of parents, and are working to help parents control their televisions, their actions do not demonstrate such concern. Though they have pledged their dedication to upholding broadcast standards, their legal departments have filed lawsuits seeking to allow them to air expletives any time, day or night. Meanwhile, they race against one another in search of "edgier" material to air—and while programming later in prime time becomes raunchier, more and more seeps, or is pushed, into the family hour [8:00–9:00 p.m.]. Though they have promoted multimillion-dollar campaigns to highlight parental controls based on content ratings and the V-chip, parents have found such tools useless. As shown in previously published Parents Television Council studies, the TV ratings are confusing to parents and are applied inconsistently by the networks. Truly, the fox is guarding the henhouse.

Parents Television Council,
"The Alarming Family Hour . . . No Place for Children,"
September 5, 2007.

media has similar effects when viewed in home or community settings and whether such exposure has long-term consequences.

Research involving the Children in the Community study addressed these limitations and demonstrated a relationship between consistent consumption of media (3 hours a day) in the home/community and an increased likelihood of aggression toward others. Researchers followed 707 families for a 17-year period and examined the relationship between consumption of media and aggression, using youth self-report, parental report, and criminal arrest data. Forty-two percent of males who viewed television more than 3 hours per day at age 14 were reported to have been involved in aggressive acts that resulted in injury when they were 16 or 22 years old; this compared to 9% of males who viewed less than 1 hour of television per day. This relationship persisted even after controlling for other factors such as prior history of aggressive behavior, child neglect, neighborhood violence, family income, psychiatric disorders, and gender.

Exploring Explanations

Social learning theory provides an explanation for how violent media may influence childhood aggression. Social learning theory posits that a child learns how to act and forms his or her attitudes from observing important role models in his or her life. Characters portrayed in the media may become models that influence the child's attitudes, beliefs, and behavior. He or she may learn to see violence as a part of everyday life and an acceptable way to solve interpersonal problems. Because violence in the media is so frequently presented without negative consequences, youth may fail to accurately assess or even understand the real-life consequences of violent actions against others. Children 7 years and younger do not understand the difference between reality and fantasy, according to research. Developmentally, they are less able to discern reality from fantasy and are more likely to be emotionally and cognitively affected by the violence they observe.

Finally, the effects of violent media appear to be race-, class-, and gender-blind. Violent media influences both males and females (although some data suggest that males may be slightly more affected), and while some studies suggest a connection between socioeconomic and community factors and vulnerability to the effects of media violence, most research shows that all groups can experience the effects of media violence on attitudes and behaviors.

Promising Strategies

At present, little research exists on the effectiveness of different interventions for reducing the effects of violent media on children. Some commonsense approaches such as limiting children's access to violent media and teaching them to be informed media consumers have gained support from professional and legislative groups. Despite the lack of research, available interventions have both intuitive and theoretical appeal.

Researchers have found that limiting media consumption, including television viewing and video game playing, can reduce short-term aggressiveness in children. Since the majority of children's media exposure occurs in the home, parents/caretakers play a pivotal role in limiting consumption both by monitoring their child's viewing habits and by regulating what and how much media they consume. Parents/guardians should engage their children in discussion of this issue but realize that they may not share their children's opinions or interpretations of violent programming and content.

In 1996 Congress passed the Telecommunications Act, which was intended to assist parents and caregivers in reducing children's exposure to violent media. The legislation calls for the inclusion of V-chips in all new televisions and for the development of a rating system to enable parents/caretakers to assess the violence content of specific shows. The ratings system, however, is voluntary and networks are allowed to rate their own shows. To some extent, the industry is responding with devices such as Weemote and TVGuardian, which can filter out certain television channels and even offensive language, thereby providing some level of parental control over children's viewing preferences.

Another strategy to reduce the effects of violent media is media literacy training. Parents/caregivers and children are taught to critically appraise the media they consume and develop strategies for reducing exposure to violence. They are taught to distinguish between real and fantasy violence, identify the real-life consequences of violent acts that occur in the media, critically assess the motivations of the producers in making the media product, and describe nonviolent alternatives to the violent actions contained in the programming. Despite this training, "more than half of Americans do not know their television is equipped with a V-chip and two-thirds have never used it."

Media literacy training resources include the Just Think Foundation, which focuses on children by providing educational programs that can be utilized during or after school and online; the Center for Media Literacy, which offers media literacy training for teachers, parents, and community, civic, and youth leaders through exercises and activities in small-group settings; and the American Academy of Pediatrics Media Matters program, which provides training for health care professionals in media literacy and educational materials for use in the health care setting.

| "When one looks at juvenile violence across society, exposure to media violence comes pretty low down [on] the list as a risk factor."

There Is No Evidence Suggesting Media Violence Leads to Juvenile Violence

Lancet

While studies show a short-term increase in aggression among young people exposed to violent media, there is no evidence of a long-term impact, maintain the editors of the Lancet, *a British medical journal. In fact, they claim, many factors contribute to violent behavior among youth. Indeed, they argue, poverty, domestic abuse, drug use, and mental illness are better predictors of youth violence than exposure to violent media. Since media technology is constantly evolving, and quantifying exposure to media violence is so challenging, money would be better spent identifying high-risk groups of children than seeking a particular causal factor, the authors conclude.*

"Is Exposure to Media Violence a Public-Health Risk?," *Lancet*, vol. 371, April 5–11, 2008, p. 1137. Copyright © 2008 by Elsevier. www.sciencedirect.com/science/journal /01406736.

As you read, consider the following questions:

1. According to the *Lancet* editors, what seems new about the recommendations made in the Byron report?

2. How is violence tackled in the United States, in the authors' opinion?

3. According to the authors, what type of studies would provide insight into society's concern about aggression against people and property?

For video game fans in the UK [United Kingdom], this month [April 2008] sees the release of the much anticipated *Manhunt 2* and *Grand Theft Auto IV*. The earlier versions of these so-called video nasties hit the headlines when their makers were taken to task over whether the violent nature of their games provoked real-life killings. Last week the Byron report [referring to a study conducted by Dr. Tanya Byron] was launched to a huge ministerial fanfare. It was commissioned by the UK Government in 2007, in response to increasing concerns about the risks to children's safety and well-being from exposure to harmful or inappropriate material on the Internet and in video games. The report stresses that while the Internet and video games provide educational opportunities, there are dangers: for example, exposure to extreme violence in games, and bullying over the Internet. Many of the report's recommendations already exist, such as age ratings for games, parental control software, and restrictions on illegal content online. What seems new is the shift away from the idea that more regulation is needed. Instead, the report concludes that better information and education around safety targeting parents and children is crucial.

A Closer Look

But a closer look at the evidence about the actual harm caused by the media begs the question of how much of a public-

An American Tradition

It's almost an American tradition to blame the corruption of youth on violent mass media, from the lurid "half dime" novels of the 19th century to 1930s gangster films and 1950s horror/crime comics. In 1972, a report to the U.S. surgeon general addressed the then growing concerns about violent television. Its authors pondered how television content and programming practices could be changed to reduce the risk of increasing aggression without causing other social harms. They concluded: "The state of present knowledge does not permit an agreed answer."

Violent video games are the most recent medium to be decried by researchers, politicians, and the popular press as contributing to society's ills. In particular, they were implicated in a series of notorious shootings. . . .

We might take a lesson from America's history of media hysteria. It's time to move beyond blanket condemnations and frightening anecdotes and focus on developing targeted educational and policy interventions based on solid data. As with the entertainment media of earlier generations, we may look back on some of today's games with nostalgia, and our grandchildren may wonder what the fuss was about.

Cheryl K. Olson,
"Media Violence Research and Youth Violence Data:
Why Do They Conflict?,"
Academic Psychiatry, *Summer 2004.*

health risk the exposure to violence presents. Can the current evidence provide real guidance?

The effects of violence in video games on negative behaviour in children and adolescents have been intensely studied and debated. Some studies show that violent imagery increases the likelihood of short-term aggressive or fearful behaviour, especially in boys. The effects in older children are less clear and no long-term increase in aggressiveness or violence has been shown. There is no evidence to suggest that individuals exposed to media violence go on to commit crimes. However, it is not clear whether this largely experimental research can be applied to situations in everyday life. Studies are small with nonrepresentative samples; they do not look at present-day games or measure the exposure to violence. The focus is on finding harm; evidence for actual harm is scant. Not all aggression is bad. In fact it can be quite positive. And the assumption that everyone is at risk of being violent disregards the fact that some people are more susceptible to violence and may seek out violent material.

Violent or aggressive actions seldom result from a single cause; instead multiple factors converge over time to contribute to such behaviour. When one looks at juvenile violence across society, exposure to media violence comes pretty low down [on] the list as a risk factor. Much stronger predictors include involvement in crime, poverty, family breakdown or abuse, drug use, and psychiatric illness. Most media violence research excludes the involvement of these factors and how they may interact.

The Pressure on Governments

In the USA, tackling violence is highly politicised. Most of the media violence research is led by a group of prominent US psychologists who have helped influence the health agendas of the American Medical Association and American [Academy] of Pediatrics. Researchers in the UK and Europe have been less political. The problem for governments is that they can do little about the many causes of violence, but in the wake of events like the Columbine [school] shootings [in Colorado in

1999] there is pressure on governments to be seen to be doing something; it is much easier to talk tough on media violence than it is to regulate guns.

Currently, there is simply not enough evidence to devise recommendations for public health. Perhaps it is time to give up the quest to isolate the specific contribution that media violence makes to aggression, given the complexity of other risk factors involved. Moreover, the degree of exposure to various types of violent content is hard to quantify, and longitudinal studies are hampered by constantly evolving technology.

Instead of making assumptions from sales data on what games are bought, there is a need for observational studies on what children actually play and how they play (individually and in groups). Given that violence has different cultural contexts in the way it is portrayed, studies in children from ethnic minorities would be valuable in increasing our knowledge. Attention to identifying higher-risk groups, such as children with depression and behavioural and mental health problems, and those exposed to real-world violence, could yield possible markers for abnormal behaviour. Given that aggression against people and property is what society is most concerned about, studies looking at the play patterns in juvenile offenders would provide further insight. With these kinds of data we can establish whether media violence may or may not exacerbate existing mental, psychological, or behavioural health problems. Only then should research focus on how changes in media use can reduce those risks, and not before.

"Childhood physical abuse in particular is thought to be one of the most frequent correlates of aggressive and delinquent behaviors in later life."

From Victim to Aggressor: The Cycle of Youth Violence

Dwain C. Fehon

In the following viewpoint, psychiatrist Dwain C. Fehon claims that witnessing or experiencing violence in the home is one of the most significant juvenile violence risk factors. According to the author, several psychological theories have emerged to explain the correlation. Social learning theory, for example, Fehon maintains, suggests that children in violent homes see violence as normal. Witnessing violence in the community, he asserts, further increases the risk. Since the costs of juvenile violence are so high, American communities need mental health approaches that include juvenile offenders, their families, and the community, he reasons. Fehon is a professor of psychiatry at Yale University School of Medicine and co-service manager of adolescent services at Yale-New Haven Psychiatric Hospital.

Dwain C. Fehon, "From Victim to Aggressor: The Cycle of Youth Violence," *Psychiatric Times*, vol. 24, June 2007, p. 44. Copyright © 2007 by Psychiatric Times. All rights reserved. Reproduced by permission.

As you read, consider the following questions:

1. How many children witness acts of violence in their homes each year, according to Fehon?

2. According to the author, by what age had nearly half of the victims of physical abuse and neglect in one large-scale study been arrested?

3. Into what two general categories does the author classify aggressive behaviors?

The traumatic events surrounding the recent school shootings at Virginia Tech remind us that a disturbing aspect of our current culture is the rate at which America's youth are exposed to violence. Whether it is graphic episodes of violence on television, violent music, aggressive video games, hearing about or witnessing violence in the home or neighborhood, or being the direct victim of violence—violence is a pervasive part of society that disproportionately affects youth. In fact, between 3 and 10 million children annually witness acts of violence in their homes. Of these, about 60% have been victimized multiple times by physical or sexual abuse.

Rates of child abuse and neglect in the United States range from 15 to 42 cases per 1000 children and of the 3 million cases of child abuse that are reported each year, 1 million are eventually substantiated. Similarly, as many as 60% to 70% of American youth have witnessed serious community violence, and homicide remains the second leading cause of death among youths aged 15 to 24 years. The fact that violence has become such a routine part of many children's lives raises serious concerns about the consequences of violence exposure. The issue of violence exposure and violence victimization has received considerable attention, and it is now regarded as a serious health problem affecting adolescents in nearly every sector of society.

Cycle of Violence

For decades, mental health professionals and social scientists have used the phrases "cycle of violence" and the "intergenerational transmission of violence" to describe the premise that "violence begets violence." Researchers have consistently found that children exposed to violence, either as witnesses or victims, are at high risk for having their own patterns of aggressive behavior develop. A considerable body of research points to a number of family, social, and community factors that increase the probability of violence. Specifically, family issues such as inadequate home environments, parental alcohol and drug abuse, witnessing domestic violence, and harsh parental discipline increase the risk for violent behavior in children and adolescents.

Children who are witnesses or the victims of community violence are also at increased risk for subsequent violent behavior. In addition, childhood maltreatment has a strong association with risk for violence. Childhood physical abuse in particular is thought to be one of the most frequent correlates of aggressive and delinquent behaviors in later life. For instance, in a large-scale prospective study using data taken 22 years after abuse or neglect, childhood abuse and neglect victims were significantly more likely to have been arrested for non-traffic offenses and violent crimes than non-victimized controls. Astoundingly, nearly half of the victims of physical abuse and neglect in this sample had been arrested by the age of 32.

Conceptual Models

Numerous cognitive and behavioral models have been proposed for understanding the cycle of violent and aggressive behavior. Social learning theory provides an explanation for the high violence potential observed in patients who have witnessed violence. For example, numerous studies confirm a link between observed violence and aggressive behavior in children and adolescents. These studies find that the link is an enduring one, in part because of the strength of vicarious social learning. Repeated exposure to community, domestic, or media violence is thought to promote the development of beliefs that violence and aggression are normal, acceptable responses, thereby increasing the potential to act aggressively. Furthermore, exposure to violence contributes to the development of a negativity bias, in that affected youth may exhibit more negative emotions, attribute negative intent to others, and be hypervigilant to negative stimuli.

Cicchetti and Lynch have described an ecological-transactional model to understand the process by which maltreatment occurs and development is shaped as a result of potentiating and compensatory risk factors at each level of social ecology—culture, community, and family. On the other hand, Nofziger and Kurtz have proposed a lifestyle model that focuses on the interaction between the person and his or her environment, noting that some adolescents are exposed to violence because they are involved in high-risk activities that put them at greater risk for violence exposure and subsequent victimization or perpetration. Along these lines, Stewart and colleagues found that adolescents who adopt a "code of the street" mentality actually have higher rates of victimization beyond what would be expected from living in a dangerous and disorganized neighborhood.

Impact of Violence Exposure

Studies related to the cycle of youth violence are important given the serious impact on affected individuals, communities, and society as a whole. Childhood abuse and repeated exposure to violence has a pervasive effect on a child's psychological and biological regulatory processes that can cause a complex set of reactions and lead to multiple psychiatric and functional impairments. In clinical settings, the link between

Risk Factors at Home and in the Community

	Childhood	Adolescence
Family	Low socioeconomic status/poverty	Poor parent–child relations
	Antisocial parents	Harsh, lax discipline; poor monitoring, supervision
	Poor parent–child relations	Low parental involvement
	Harsh, lax, or inconsistent discipline	Antisocial parents
	Broken home	Broken home
	Separation from parents	Low socioeconomic status/poverty
	Other conditions	Abusive parents
	Abusive parents	Other conditions
	Neglect	Family conflict (for males only)
Community		Neighborhood crime, drugs
		Neighborhood disorganization

TAKEN FROM: Department of Health and Human Services, *Youth Violence: A Report of the Surgeon General*, January 2001.

violence exposure and depression, anxiety, post-traumatic stress disorder (PTSD), drug and alcohol abuse, and aggression and delinquency are frequently observed. Numerous other problems are associated with violence exposure, including a higher suicide risk, poor academic performance, and high-risk sexual behavior. Economically, direct and indirect costs of youth violence exceed $158 billion annually.

Another important issue in understanding the impact of children's exposure to violence relates to neurological maturation and neurobiological processes in response to traumatic stress. The neurobiological sequelae of violence exposure and childhood abuse are well documented. Much of the work in this area has focused on altered catecholamine activity within the hypothalamic-pituitary-adrenal axis following exposure to traumatic events. Central catecholamine neurons play a critical role in the level of alertness, vigilance, attention, memory, fear conditioning, and cardiovascular response to life-threatening situations. Recurrent exposure to violence can lead to frequent flooding or dysregulation of noradrenergic and corticosteroid systems and contribute to heightened responsiveness and increased levels of aggression in persons with PTSD.

It is believed that these chronically dysregulated systems have an eventual impact on structural and functional brain development. Research using functional MRI and positron emission tomography points toward dysfunction of the hippocampus in patients with PTSD. The hippocampus is believed to mediate emotional processing of complex visual stimuli and the integration of different aspects of memory, as well as the ability to locate a memory in time, place, and context. Prolonged periods of stress have been shown to correlate with elevated cortisol levels in the brain, which can damage the hippocampus in humans, thus potentially affecting a person's ability to accurately process and respond to incoming information.

Accordingly, brain development, stress regulation, and exposure to early traumatic experience are seen as interactive and cumulative in their influence on the development of impulsive violence and aggression.

Psychopathology of Trauma and Impulsive Violence

Aggressive behaviors can be classified into 2 general categories: premeditated aggression and impulsive aggression. While traumatized youth who perpetuate the cycle of violence may do so for a multitude of reasons—such as a means to express anger and resentment, revenge, distrust, as a self-protective need to attack before being attacked, to escape stressful circumstances, or to reenact previously abusive relationships— youth referred for psychiatric care typically exhibit reactive, impulsive forms of aggressive behavior. Increasingly, impulsivity, affective dysregulation, hyperarousal, and cognitive disorganization are seen as key concepts in understanding the determinants of violence and aggression among traumatized youth; consideration of these elements holds promise for the implementation of effective psychiatric interventions for those referred for outpatient or inpatient psychiatric treatment. . . .

Approaches to Decrease Risk of Violence

Despite the strong association between violence victimization and later violence perpetration, not all children exposed to violence become aggressive and perpetuate the cycle of violence. Some withstand the negative effects of violence and show a pattern of resilient development. Many of the protective factors associated with decreased impact of violence exposure make intuitive sense.

Youths exposed to high levels of community violence but who live within families with high cohesion, high structure, effective parenting practices, and strong beliefs about the family are less likely to engage in violent behaviors than are youth in less well-functioning families. Supportive parent-child relationships characterized by communication, concern, and parent-connectedness have been linked to reductions in internalizing and externalizing behavior, including PTSD and aggression. Programs that build school safety also enhance adaptive functioning at school under conditions of high violence exposure. Thus, while supportive families, peers, and schools may not prevent an individual from being exposed to violence, they can indeed protect against the risk of subsequent emotional maladjustment, including the risk of violence.

Along these lines, community-based intervention programs in which mental health clinicians work side by side with police departments to rapidly respond to incidents of community violence have been shown to be especially helpful in addressing the emotional impact of traumatic violence. Therefore, interventions that involve an integrated approach that includes available family, school, and community supports would seem to be most likely to reduce the risk of violence among traumatized/violence-exposed youth.

Once an adolescent is referred for mental health treatment because of impulsive aggressive behavior, a range of therapeutic options are available. Individual cognitive-behavioral therapy can be an effective method of improving problem-solving skills and social-skill deficits. Dialectical behavior therapy may decrease internalizing and externalizing symptoms such as anger and depression in adolescents. Group therapy offers peer support and validation for one's reaction to traumatic events. Family therapy offers an emotionally neutral forum to discuss the antecedents and consequences of aggressive behavior in the home, and it is a link to the intergenerational transmission of violence.

Psychopharmacological therapies may also reduce symptoms of hyperarousal and impulsivity associated with PTSD, yet knowledge of medication treatments targeting aggression for children and adolescents is limited by a lack of reliable, well-controlled clinical trials. The FDA has yet to approve medication for pediatric use targeting PTSD or aggression. . . .

Given the rate at which America's youth are exposed to violence, mental health providers are encouraged to develop effective treatments that decrease the victim-to-perpetrator cycle of violence. Adolescents who exhibit symptoms of impulsive aggression are likely to lack prerequisite affect regulation skills to modulate aggressive impulses and will require integrated psychopharmacological and behavioral strategies to improve affect regulation and behavioral control. Approaches that integrate individual, family, community-based, and psychopharmacological interventions are required to address the pervasive and deleterious effects of violence exposure and childhood abuse.

> *"Children of divorced parents are up to
> six times more likely to be delinquent
> than children from intact families."*

Juvenile Crime Is More Likely in Single-Parent Families

Curt Alfrey

*Criminal defense attorney Curt Alfrey argues in the following
viewpoint that children raised in single-parent homes are much
more likely to end up in jail, while children in homes with married parents and little conflict are less likely to become involved
in the juvenile justice system. Children in intact families tend to
receive more supervision and are thus less likely to get into
trouble, Alfrey asserts. Moreover, he claims, economic situations
sometimes force single-parent families into higher-crime neighborhoods, where school officials and law enforcement may more
readily treat the children as delinquents. Strengthening family
relationships and enhancing families will therefore help reduce
the incidence of juvenile crime, Alfrey reasons.*

Curt Alfrey, "Juvenile Delinquency and Family Structure: Implications for Marriage and
Relationship Education," National Healthy Marriage Resource Center, January 1, 2009.
www.healthymarriageinfo.org. Copyright © 2009 by National Healthy Marriage Resource Center. All rights reserved. Reproduced by permission.

As you read, consider the following questions:

1. How much does Alfrey claim is spent annually on federal, state, and local juvenile justice systems?

2. What does the author assert is true of students attending schools with a higher proportion of single-parent families?

3. In the author's view, what is gang membership possibly a result of, as historically identified in literature?

Juvenile delinquency is of perpetual concern in the United States. In 2007, law enforcement agencies reported 2.18 million arrests of juveniles (persons under age 18). There are two types of delinquency offenses. The first type of offense is a behavior that would be a criminal law violation for an adult. The other offense is called a "status" offense. Status offenses are delinquent actions that do not apply to adults, like running away and truancy. They make up only 5 percent of the offenses of juveniles in custody. The other 95 percent of juveniles in custody at any point in time (excluding those in adult prisons) are held for criminal delinquency offenses.

The Types and Costs of Juvenile Crime

The types of crimes committed by juveniles are compiled through self-reporting or from reports provided by the juvenile justice system. Juvenile delinquent behavior is believed to be underrepresented due to the limited methods of collecting juvenile crime data. Juvenile arrests accounted for 16 percent of all violent crime arrests (i.e., murder, rape, assault) and 26 percent of all property crime arrests (i.e., burglary, theft, arson). Other crimes for which juveniles are arrested include simple assault, vandalism, gambling, disorderly conduct, weapons possession, illicit drug/liquor violation (including DUI [driving under the influence of alcohol or drugs]) and prostitution. It is important to note that a number of misdemeanor crimes go unreported while serious crimes involving injury and/or large economic loss are reported more often.

It is estimated that $14.4 billion is spent annually on the federal, state and local juvenile justice systems. This includes the costs of law enforcement and the courts, detention, residential placement, incarceration and substance abuse treatment. However, this figure does not include the costs of probation, physical and mental health care services, child welfare and family services, school costs and the costs to victims. It is estimated that combined, spending on juvenile justice could exceed $28.8 billion.

The Gang Problem

Gang membership among juveniles has become a major issue over the past few decades in regards to juvenile delinquency. Concurrent with the reemergence of youth gangs in the 1980s and 1990s (after a hiatus in the 1970s), the juvenile homicide rate doubled. According to the Office of Juvenile Justice and Delinquency Prevention (2000), to be considered a gang, a group must have more than two members and the members must fall within the age range of 12–24. The group must also show some stability (as opposed to transient youth groups), and a central element of the group is involvement in criminal activity. It is the criminal activity that separates gangs from other youth groups (like school clubs) that would otherwise meet the criteria.

Members of youth gangs are more likely to engage in delinquent behavior than their peers. In 2007, youth gang membership was estimated at 788,000 and total youth gangs at 27,000. This represents a resurgence in gang activity following a marked decline from the mid-1990s to the early 2000s. Data compiled from self-reporting by gang members in urban areas shows that gang members are three times more likely to say they had been arrested and five times more likely to report they had sold drugs. In various surveys in urban areas across the U.S., gang members reported being three times more likely than non-gang members (not in the juvenile justice system) their age to commit break-ins and assaults, four times more likely to commit felony thefts, and eight times more likely to commit robberies.

Family Structure and Juvenile Crime

Investigation into the cause of juvenile delinquency shows that there is an association between family structure and the criminal behavior of these minors, even when socioeconomic status is controlled. The Bureau of Justice Statistics found that 72 percent of jailed juveniles come from a fragmented family. Policy makers are beginning to recognize the link between family structure and juvenile crime. For example, a study conducted in Wisconsin found that the incarceration rate for children of divorced parents was 12 times higher than for children in two-parent families. . . .

A 1998 U.S. longitudinal study tracking over 6,400 boys for over 20 years found that children who grew up without their biological father in the home were roughly three times more likely to commit a crime that led to incarceration than children from intact families. Others have found that children of divorced parents are up to six times more likely to be delinquent than children from intact families. Boys raised without their fathers were more than twice as likely to end up in jail as those raised with their fathers, and 70% of incarcerated adults come from single-parent homes.

A 2005 policy brief from the Institute for Marriage and Public Policy (IMAPP) found that both the individual risk and overall rates of crime were reduced when parents were married. The brief summarized 23 U.S. studies published in peer-reviewed journals between 2000 and 2005, and determined that areas with high rates of family fragmentation (especially unwed childbearing) tended to have higher rates of crime. In addition, they found evidence that teens raised in single-parent homes were more likely to commit crimes. In one study [authored by T.M. Franke], adolescents in single-parent and kinship families were "significantly more likely than adolescents in intact families to report having been in a serious physical fight in the past year, to have seriously injured someone in the past year, and to have shot or stabbed someone in the past year; they were almost two and three times more likely to have pulled a knife or a gun on someone in the past year."

Beyond a youth's immediate family, the prevalence of two-parent families in the community appears to influence the likelihood of juvenile delinquency. A study from the *Journal of Criminal Justice* looked not only at the individual juvenile's family structure, but also at the structures of those with whom the juvenile interacted to determine the frequency with which an individual juvenile committed delinquent acts. In a nonrandom sample of 4,671 eighth graders drawn from 35 schools in ten cities that offered the Gang Resistance Education and Training program, they found that adolescents who were living in a single-parent family were at a significantly higher risk for delinquency than those adolescents living with two parents. These elevated rates held true for juvenile crimes involving both property and violent crime indexes, in addition to status juvenile crimes.

Students attending schools with a higher proportion of single-parent families also had significantly higher rates of violent offenses than students attending schools where more students came from two-parent families.

Marital Quality and Juvenile Crime

Families characterized by warm interpersonal relationships and effective parenting are associated with a lower likelihood of affiliation with juvenile offenders and of juvenile crime. Similarly, children raised by married parents with low-conflict marriages are better off emotionally. Where there is a high level of marital discord, considerable conflict, inadequate supervision and violence, children are more likely to become delinquent.

When there is one parent living in the home as opposed to two, it is more difficult to supervise children all the time. Everyday activities like errands and work must be completed by the parent, which leaves no parent in the home. Because of this, children in single-parent homes tend to receive lower levels of supervision. There is a strong correlation between lack of parental supervision and an increased likelihood of juvenile substance abuse, criminality and delinquency.

Although demographic characteristics alone cannot explain gang affiliation, family structure has long been considered integral to understanding gang behavior. For example, gang membership historically was identified in literature as a possible result of identity problems for young men when a male role model was not in the home. Empirical evidence shows that minority youth residing in single-parent households are at a greater risk for joining gangs than white youth from two-parent households. Several researchers [as explained by W. Reed and S. Decker] have suggested that "the gang can serve as a surrogate extended family for adolescents who do not see their own families as meeting their needs for belonging, nurturance and acceptance." Family problems were cited as one of the major distinguishing factors for females who were members of gangs versus those who were not.

The Implications

It is important to consider the context of the relationship between family structure and juvenile delinquency. Single-parent families often are financially vulnerable as compared to married households. In turn, these economic circumstances frequently draw these families into more affordable but "bad" neighborhoods. School officials, the police, the courts and the "system," respond and react to children of these homes in ways that identify them as delinquents.

Children growing up with two attentive, involved biological parents in a healthy, low-conflict marriage are more likely to experience an overall sense of well-being and less likely to become delinquent as opposed to children growing up in other circumstances.

The greatest opportunity to prevent juvenile substance abuse and crime can be found within our families. Strong and positive families have an early and sustained impact on reducing substance abuse, increasing school bonding and academic performance, dealing with conduct disorders, avoiding delinquent peers and reducing juvenile crime. The most critical family characteristics that help youth avoid associations with delinquent peers are parental supervision and monitoring, as well as parental care and support. Interventions designed to reduce family conflict, increase family involvement, and improve parental monitoring have been shown to reduce juvenile substance abuse and crime.

Research makes clear that the potential for future juvenile delinquency among youths can be significantly diminished by providing parents and juveniles with skills for relationship strengthening, personal growth and family enhancement.

| *"The great majority of school shootings are perpetrated by victims of bullying."*

Bullying Contributes to School Shootings

Izzy Kalman

Bullying is increasing among students in schools nationwide, maintains Izzy Kalman in the following viewpoint. Although some news media have painted a portrait of school shooters such as Eric Harris and Dylan Klebold as bullies rather than victims, Kalman insists that school shooters do not commit mass killings because they want to bully people, but because they feel like victims. To fight bullying, Kalman argues that we must understand that we are all bullies and victims, it just depends from whose point of view we are looking. Izzy Kalman is a nationally certified school psychologist who has been working in schools and private practice since 1978. He is the author of Bullies to Buddies: How to Turn Your Enemies into Friends *and other publications for dealing with bullying and relationship problems.*

As you read, consider the following questions:

1. According to the author, Columbine launched the modern world's war against what?

2. How does the author describe Columbine shooters Eric Harris and Dylan Klebold?

3. Why is feeling victimized dangerous, in the author's view?

I'm [writing] this [viewpoint] a couple of weeks after the tenth anniversary of the Columbine [school] shooting. That date—April 20—is important to me because the Columbine shooting was the event that made me realize my mission to teach the world a better way to understand and deal with the problem of bullying. I never expected this mission to be such a difficult one, and so far I have been far from successful. Even though schools are actually the safest place for kids to be, far safer than their own homes, the anti-bully witch hunt has been so phenomenally successful that bullying in school has become the biggest fear of parents. In the weeks since the Columbine anniversary, the media has bombarded us with horrible stories about victims of bullying taking their own lives, causing the public to continue growing in fear and loathing of bullies.

Most School Shooters Are Victims of Bullying

As most of you are aware, Columbine launched the modern world's war against bullies. Our experts concluded that since the great majority of school shootings are perpetrated by victims of bullying, we need to get rid of bullies. If we can only make bullies disappear, no kids will be victims, and no one will have any motivation to shoot up their schools. So with ten years of massive anti-bully education, why is bullying becoming a more intensive problem? Why isn't it going down?

In case you have been oblivious to recent news, the month-and-a-half period preceding the tenth Columbine anniversary had more high-profile mass shootings than any six-week period in history. The most horrific took place in the city of

Binghamton, New York, where my own son happens to go to college. Without exception, every one of these shootings was committed by someone feeling like a victim . . . of their ex-spouse, of their boss, of other students, of the economy. Why are so many people going on angry shooting rampages?

Of course the following cannot be the only explanation for these shootings, because each shooter has his own history, constitution and motives, but the massive anti-bully education we have been getting since Columbine can only have served to contribute to people's anger towards, and desire for revenge against, their perceived bullies. After years of hearing endlessly that bullies are incredibly dangerous, that bullies shouldn't be tolerated, that bullies should be punished and expelled, and that society must protect us from bullies, is it any wonder that some of us eventually crack when society fails to protect us from bullies, and pick up guns to solve our problems once and for all?

(Before I continue, I must ask you to please refrain from making the ridiculous complaint that I am "pro-bully" and "anti-victim." No one cares about victims more than I do. But "bully" and "victim" are not objective diagnoses. They are subjective experiences. We are all bullies and victims. It just depends whose point of view we are looking from. Whenever we are angry at people, we feel we are their victims, but they are likely to feel we are their bullies.)

Feeling Like a Victim

Amazingly, no matter how many events are screaming in our faces, "PEOPLE WHO COMMIT HORRIFIC ACTS FEEL LIKE VICTIMS," we refuse to get the message and intensify our campaign against bullies. Even though Columbine woke up the modern world to the plight of victims of bullying, since Eric Harris and Dylan Klebold so dramatically portrayed themselves as victims, there has been a strong—and blazingly successful—attempt to re-characterize the Columbine killers as bullies rather than victims. There is a good chance you happened across the following news story, which the media bombarded us with in honor of the tenth Columbine anniversary, informing the world that the Columbine killers were not victims at all, but bullies.

The anti-bully establishment couldn't have been happier with this story. The idea that Harris and Klebold are victims has been a thorn in the side of the anti-bully movement. Victims are supposed to be saintly innocents who need protection, and bullies are supposed to be cold, cowardly psychopaths who pick on the weak. But how can victims be angelic when they can commit horrific school shootings? What a relief, then, to discover that these monsters were after all, bullies, and not victims. With this new characterization of the Columbine killers as bullies, we can continue on our anti-bully witch hunt unencumbered by doubt.

The article talks about a new book, *Columbine*, by Dave Cullen. The book paints the Columbine killers as full of rage; paranoid; cold-blooded, predatory psychopaths; and super-terrorists. This sure makes them sound like bullies.

But paranoia is not a bully feeling. Paranoia, the feeling that everyone is against us, is the ultimate victim feeling. Being a psychopath and feeling like a victim are not mutually exclusive. If a psychopath feels victimized by you, you had better watch out!

Raging Against Those at the Top

Rage is not a bully feeling; we go into a rage when we feel victimized.

Terrorists feel like victims; they want revenge against the great powers that have victimized their people.

No one commits mass shootings and then turns their guns on themselves because they want to bully people. They do it

The Effects of Bullying

Bullying has serious and lasting effects. . . . Research has found bullying has significant effects for those who are bullied, those who bully others, and those who witness bullying.

People Who Are Bullied:

- Have higher risk of depression and anxiety, including the following symptoms, that may persist into adulthood:

    Increased feelings of sadness and loneliness

    Changes in sleep and eating patterns

    Loss of interest in activities

- Have increased thoughts about suicide that may persist into adulthood. In one study, adults who recalled being bullied in youth were 3 times more likely to have suicidal thoughts or inclinations.

- Are more likely to have health complaints. In one study, being bullied was associated with physical health status 3 years later.

- Have decreased academic achievement (GPA [grade point average] and standardized test scores) and school participation.

- Are more likely to miss, skip, or drop out of school.

- Are more likely to retaliate through extremely violent measures. In 12 of 15 school shooting cases in the 1990s, the shooters had a history of being bullied.

"Effects of Bullying,"
StopBullying.gov, 2012. www.stopbullying.gov.

because they feel like victims. (Again, I am not "anti-victim." The bullies and victims are us, and we are most dangerous when we feel like victims.)

The article says about this new book: "It's a portrait of Harris and Klebold as a sort of *In Cold Blood* criminal duo—a deeply disturbed, suicidal pair who over more than a year psyched each other up for an Oklahoma City–style terrorist bombing, an apolitical, over-the-top revenge fantasy against years of snubs, slights and cruelties, real and imagined."

"Revenge fantasy against years of snubs, slights and cruelties, real and imagined." Is this the thinking of people who feel like bullies or victims?

By the way, have you read the terrific book, *In Cold Blood*, by Truman Capote? It contains the psychiatrist's lengthy description of Perry Edward Smith, the member of the pair of robbers who committed the horrific killings. It is a perfect depiction of a person with a victim mentality.

Eric Harris and Dylan Klebold

The article goes on to say about Eric Harris: "One of Harris' last journal entries read: 'I hate you people for leaving me out of so many fun things. And no don't . . . say, "Well that's your fault," because it isn't, you people had my phone #, and I asked and all, but no. No no no don't let the weird-looking Eric KID come along.'"

Are these the words of someone who feels like a bully or a victim?

It says about Dylan Klebold: "Klebold, on the other hand, was anxious and lovelorn, summing up his life at one point in his journal as 'the most miserable existence in the history of time.'"

And: "Klebold also was paranoid. 'I have always been hated, by everyone and everything,' he wrote."

Are these descriptions of someone who feels like a bully or a victim?

The article says: "The U.S. Secret Service and U.S. Education Department soon began studying school shooters. In 2002, researchers presented their first findings: School shooters, they said, followed no set profile, but most were depressed and felt persecuted."

"Felt persecuted." Bully feeling or victim feeling?

How many shootings will it take before we learn that we are most dangerous not when we feel like bullies but when we feel like victims? Will we never learn?

"The laws and programs designed to en-sure [a school shooting like the one at Columbine] would never happen again were based on shaky foundations."

Blaming School Shootings on Bullying Can Cause More Harm than Good

Kay S. Hymowitz

In the following viewpoint, Kay S. Hymowitz claims that nation-wide anti-bullying programs and policies designed to prevent an-other school shooting such as the one at Columbine High School are based on widely accepted myths about the shooting. Experts have shown that the Columbine shooters, Eric Harris and Dylan Klebold, were not driven to murder because they were outcast victims of bullying; rather, they suffered from mental illnesses that drove them to kill. Moreover, Hymowitz argues, unproven anti-bullying programs create wasteful and ineffective bureau-cracies to address concerns that are the responsibility of parents and educators. Hymowitz is a fellow at the Manhattan Institute for Policy Research, a free-market think tank.

Kay S. Hymowitz, "Columbine's Long-Term Harm: The Bully Pulpit," *Youth Today*, November 1, 2009, p. 21. Copyright © 2009 by Youth Today. All rights reserved. Reproduced by permission.

As you read, consider the following questions:

1. According to the viewpoint, what was the widely accepted conclusion following the Columbine shooting that emerged from reports about the "Trench Coat Mafia"?

2. How many state legislatures passed laws requiring schools to ban bullying, according to the author?

3. What does research published in the 2007 *Criminal Justice Review* conclude about anti-bullying programs?

Like 9/11 [referring to the September 11, 2001, terrorist attacks on the United States], Columbine [referring to the 1999 school shooting in a high school in Colorado] was an event that "changed everything." It challenged our belief that kids, for all their quirks, would always conform to basic rules of human nature. Now, as we mark the 10th anniversary of the massacre of 13 and suicide of two that took place in the high school [in Colorado] in April 1999, a troubling cautionary lesson for educators, youth workers and policy makers is coming into focus.

Shaky Theories of Columbine's Causes

It turns out that a lot of what we thought caused Eric Harris and Dylan Klebold to kill and maim so many was wrong— and that the laws and programs designed to ensure it would never happen again were based on shaky foundations. Almost immediately after the killings, news stories described a school environment dominated by athlete-bullies.

"Columbine High School is a culture where initiation rituals meant upper-class wrestlers twisted the nipples of freshman wrestlers until they turned purple and tennis players sent hard volleys to younger teammates' backsides," the *Washington Post* reported just a few months after the event. "All of it angered and oppressed Eric Harris and Dylan Klebold, leading to the April day when they staged their murderous rampage here, killing 13 and wounding 21."

Other reports told about the "Trench Coat Mafia," a group of outsiders, including Klebold and Harris, who wore black trench coats and plotted revenge against these alleged tormentors. The widely accepted conclusion: A toxic school culture dominated by bullies made them do it.

The theory launched thousands of anti-bullying conferences, grant applications, curricula, programs, workshops and videos, along with the careers of researchers and consultants. Even the most hard-stretched communities somehow found the funds to get at the putative root cause of school violence. No one has calculated precisely how much federal and local money went into this bully-educational complex, but it's safe to say it was many millions of taxpayer dollars. Less expensive but equally certain of their rightness that bullying explained Columbine were the 44 state legislatures that passed laws requiring schools to ban bullying.

A Different Theory About Columbine

There was just one problem: Bullying had nothing to do with the Colorado tragedy.

According to Dave Cullen, author of a best-selling book, *Columbine*, the killers had plenty of friends and were not even part of the mild-mannered Trench Coat Mafia. After combing through records that could fill a high school football field, both Cullen and Peter Langman, author of *Why Kids Kill* and clinical director of KidsPeace, a charity providing treatment for disturbed children, concluded that the only bully connected to the horror was Eric Harris himself; it seems that Harris had repeatedly threatened his classmate Brooks Brown.

According to Cullen and Langman, the real explanation for the tragedy was mental illness. Harris was a raging psychopath and Klebold a suicidal depressive.

It could be argued that even if people got the Columbine story wrong, there was no harm done. After all, bullying is a problem wherever kids congregate, and especially in the schools. According to the Indicators of School Crime and Safety 2008 survey from the National Center for Education Statistics, 32 percent of students said they had been bullied during the previous year. In bad cases, kids are in despair, their grades suffer, and they avoid going to school. In extreme instances, they might even try to kill themselves. Why not introduce programs and laws to tackle the problem?

The Problem with Bullying Programs

Two reasons.

First, it's not clear that the laws and programs work. Most of the research evaluating those programs is seriously flawed. But a meta-analysis of rigorous research published in 2007 in *Criminal Justice Review* found that "anti-bullying programs produced little discernible effect on youth participants."

Reason No. 2 might explain why: Bullying programs bureaucratize and systematize what should be the commonsense efforts of adults to socialize kids. Adults working with youth have a responsibility to teach them to suppress their natural tendencies toward status-seeking and cruelty. Turning that behavior into a legal matter to be resolved through some bureaucratic process can't help with such a delicate human task. Instead of reacting to cruelty, the educator consults his rule book, calls his lawyer and forgoes judgment.

The bullying bureaucracy also imposes a rigid, conceptual structure on behavior that does not fit into neat categories. *Good Morning America* recently reported that over the past 10 years, senior girls at New Jersey's Millburn High School have created a "slut list" of incoming freshmen girls. Every adult knows this is wrong. Instead of consulting the guidebook about whether to call it bullying and push kids into programs of uncertain value, why not do the obvious: Denounce and, if feasible, punish the behavior?

For better or worse, Americans are suspicious of bureaucratic expertise. Unfortunately, the bully-educational complex, founded on faulty premises, plagued by arbitrary nomenclature, and very possibly a waste of taxpayer money, gives them more reason for doubt.

Periodical and Internet Sources Bibliography

The following articles have been selected to supplement the diverse views presented in this chapter.

Kimberly Bender, Stephen Tripodi, Jemel Aguilar, and Sanna Thompson	"Predicting Arrest in Early Adulthood: The Relationship Between Internal and External Sources of Control," *Social Work Research*, March 2010.
Elizabeth Brown and Mike Males	"Does Age or Poverty Level Best Predict Criminal Arrest and Homicide Rates? A Preliminary Investigation," *Justice Policy Journal*, Spring 2011.
Vivien Carli	*The Media, Crime Prevention and Urban Safety: A Brief Discussion on Media Influence and Areas for Further Exploration*, International Centre for the Prevention of Crime, December 2008. www.crime-prevention-intl.org.
FBI Law Enforcement Bulletin	"Girls' Delinquency," June 2011.
Christopher J. Ferguson	"Violent Video Games: Dogma, Fear, and Pseudoscience," *Skeptical Inquirer*, September–October 2009.
Amruta Ghanekar and Sara Taveras	"MIMIC: Tackling the Root Causes of Juvenile Delinquency," *Philadelphia Social Innovations Journal*, February 2010.
Allan M. Hoffman	"Combating the Culture of Media Violence," *Pediatrics for Parents*, May–June 2011.
Lancaster New Era	"School Violence, Real or Imagined," October 9, 2008. http://lancasteronline.com.
Mary Brophy Marcus	"What Causes a Young Person to Snap?," *USA Today*, January 10, 2011.

How Should the Criminal Justice System Treat Juvenile Offenders?

Chapter Preface

One of the most hotly debated public policies is whether juveniles should be tried as adults. Supporters claim that juveniles who commit particularly brutal crimes should be held accountable and that trying and punishing them as adults will protect public safety. Opponents claim that treating juveniles as adults actually threatens public safety and does more harm than good. One of several controversies within this debate is whether juvenile brain physiology makes juveniles more prone to the poor judgment that can lead to crime and whether this physiology means they should be exempt from prosecution as adults.

Youth advocates argue that juveniles should not be treated like adults, because they do not think like adults. Indeed, brain scan research supports this claim. This view played an important role in the Supreme Court's 2005 decision in *Roper v. Simmons*, which banned the death penalty for juveniles under eighteen. According to Physicians for Human Rights, who submitted a brief in the case, "When children find themselves in emotionally charged situations, the parts of the brain that regulate emotion rather than reasoning, are more likely to be engaged."[1] Brain scans using magnetic resonance imaging, a technology used to detect tumors and other brain abnormalities, reveal that adolescent behavior is often controlled by the primitive brain, which includes the amygdala, the area that regulates fear, aggression, and impulse. As people mature, so does the prefrontal cortex, which governs reasoning and the understanding of consequences. According to Physicians for Human Rights, the prefrontal cortex does not fully develop until a person is in his or her twenties. While the Supreme Court did not directly address brain development in its deci-

---

1. "Adolescent Brain Development: A Critical Factor in Juvenile Justice Reform," Physicians for Human Rights.

sion, it agreed that juveniles do not think like adults. The majority in *Roper v. Simmons* recognized several differences between juveniles and adults, including a lack of maturity and an underdeveloped sense of responsibility that lead to impetuous and ill-considered actions and decisions. Justice Anthony Kennedy concluded, "Retribution is not proportional if the law's most severe penalty is imposed on one whose culpability or blameworthiness is diminished, to a substantial degree, by reason of youth and immaturity."[2]

Commentators who support trying juveniles as adults counter that the reasoning of the court in *Roper v. Simmons* regarding juveniles being subject to the death penalty should not be applied when deciding whether to try a juvenile as an adult in other criminal justice contexts. Prosecutor James C. Backstrom, one of the leading proponents of trying juveniles as adults, asserts, "I think a 16- or 17-year-old youth is fully capable of understanding right from wrong, and understanding that it's wrong to murder, rape or torture someone."[3] Indeed, in his dissent in *Roper v. Simmons*, Justice Antonin Scalia reasserted his reasoning in a previous case; he argues that it is "absurd to think that one must be mature enough to drive carefully, to drink responsibly, or to vote intelligently, in order to be mature enough to understand that murdering another human being is profoundly wrong, and to conform one's conduct to that most minimal of all civilized standards."[4]

Youth advocates and prosecutors continue to contest whether the nature of adolescent brains is relevant to the issue of their accountability in the criminal justice system—whether adolescent biology leads to poor decision making and, at times, criminal behavior. The authors in the chapter that follows address several aspects of the debate over how juveniles

---

2. *Roper v. Simmons*, 543 US 551 (2005), http://supremejustia.com.
3. Peter Katel, "Juvenile Justice," *CQ Researcher*, November 7, 2008.
4. *Stanford v. Kentucky*, 492 US 361 (1989) in *Roper v. Simmons, op cit.*

should be treated by the criminal justice system, highlighting the complexity of dealing with those who straddle the gap between childhood and adulthood.

> "Prosecuting juvenile offenders in adult
> court is appropriate and necessary in
> certain cases to protect public safety
> and hold youth appropriately account-
> able for their crimes."

The Criminal Justice System Should Treat Some Juveniles as Adults

James C. Backstrom

In the following viewpoint, James C. Backstrom argues that to protect public safety and hold youth accountable for serious crimes, some juveniles should be prosecuted as adults. Critics wrongly claim that prosecutors and judges are prosecuting juveniles as adults for minor offenses when in fact the very small percentage of juveniles tried as adults have typically committed serious and violent crimes. Moreover, Backstrom concludes, despite the suggestion that young people should not be prosecuted as adults because their brains are not fully developed, most juveniles do know the difference between right and wrong. Back-

strom, a county attorney in Hastings, Minnesota, is a board member of the National District Attorneys Association and co-chair of its juvenile justice committee.

As you read, consider the following questions:

1. According to Backstrom, from where do statistics that large numbers of youth are being prosecuted as adults for low-level offenses come?

2. How does the author define "blended sentencing"?

3. What are some of the mitigating factors that the author claims prosecutors and judges consider?

Prosecuting juvenile offenders in adult court is appropriate and necessary in certain cases to protect public safety and hold youth appropriately accountable for their crimes. Contrary to the claims of opponents, this sanction is not being overused by America's prosecutors. Few jurisdictions in our country prosecute more than 1–2% of juvenile offenders as adults. This is a tool reserved for the most serious, violent and chronic offenders who rightfully should face more serious consequences for their crimes than those available in juvenile court.

Don't be misled by claims that large numbers of youth are being prosecuted as adults for low level offenses, as these statistics come from the 13 states in America where laws classify 16- or 17-year-olds as adults for purposes of any prosecution. This has nothing to do with transferring juveniles to adult court. Another misapplied fact in this debate relates to the development of the human brain. Recent scientific studies have shown that in most persons the brain is not fully developed until the early to mid-20s, and the last portion of the brain to reach full maturity is the frontal lobe, which governs impulse control. While this may well explain why some youth lack the reasoning ability to fully appreciate the consequences of their actions, this does not mean that they should not be held appropriately accountable for the crimes they commit. The vast majority of teenagers understand the difference between right and wrong and know it is wrong to torture or kill someone. This is why our laws rightfully allow adult court prosecution for these and other violent crimes.

Enforcing Fair Juvenile Codes

Juveniles who commit serious and violent crimes, particularly older youth, should face potential adult court sanctions. So, too, must this remedy be available for youth who have committed less serious felonies who have a long history of convictions for which no juvenile court disposition has been effective. About one-third of our states also appropriately utilize "blended sentencing" models which combine both juvenile and adult criminal sanctions for serious, violent or habitual juvenile offenders whose crimes have been determined by either a prosecutor or a judge to not warrant immediate prosecution in adult court.

Prosecutors and judges thoughtfully and professionally enforce juvenile codes across America with fairness and impartiality every day, taking into consideration both mitigating factors, such as a juvenile offender's age and maturity and amenability to treatment and probation, and aggravating factors, such as the severity of the crime, the threat to public safety, the impact upon the victim and the offender's criminal history. After properly weighing these factors, in some cases the difficult decision to prosecute a juvenile offender as an adult is warranted.

"Policies that send youth to the adult criminal justice system . . . are 'counterproductive for the purpose of reducing violence and enhancing public safety.'"

Placing Juveniles in the Adult Criminal Justice System Is Counterproductive

Campaign for Youth Justice

In the following viewpoint, Campaign for Youth Justice (CFYJ), an organization whose goal is to end the practice of trying, sentencing, and incarcerating youth under eighteen in the adult criminal justice system, argues that youth are not safe in adult jails. Moreover, the organization asserts, adult jails do not provide the necessary education and training adolescents need. In fact, placing juveniles in adult jails increases the likelihood that they will later be rearrested for more serious crimes. Thus, the organization reasons, the practice of prosecuting juveniles as adults decreases public safety and should be abandoned.

As you read, consider the following questions:

1. What percentage of youth under eighteen were victims of sexual violence in jails, according to 2005 and 2006 data from the Bureau of Justice Statistics?

2. How long are some juveniles incarcerated in adult jails when they ultimately do not receive adult convictions, according to CFYJ?

3. In the author's view, what was the purpose of the Juvenile Justice and Delinquency Prevention Act?

Every day in America, an average of 7,500 youth are incarcerated in adult jails. The annual number of youth who are placed in adult jails is even higher—ten or twenty times the daily average according to some researchers—to account for the "turnover rate" of youth entering and exiting adult jails. Despite the life-altering consequences of incarceration in an adult jail, relatively little attention has been given to these youth. . . .

Putting Youth at Risk

It is extremely difficult to keep youth safe in adult jails. When youth are placed with adults in jails, youth are at great risk of physical and sexual assault. For example, according to the U.S. Department of Justice Bureau of Justice Statistics (BJS) in 2005 and 2006, 21% and 13% respectively, of the victims of inmate-on-inmate sexual violence in jails were youth under the age of 18—a surprisingly high percentage of victims considering that only 1% of all jail inmates are juveniles.

Recognizing the risks to youth in jails, some jailers separate youth from adult inmates. However, this is not an adequate solution either. Separating youth from adults in jail can reduce the physical or emotional harm that may result from contact with adult offenders, but unfortunately these youth are then often placed in isolation, a dangerous setting for

By Mike Keefe, politicalcartoons.com.

youth. Youth in isolation are frequently locked down 23 hours a day in small cells with no natural light. Even limited exposure to such an environment can cause anxiety, paranoia, exacerbate existing mental disorders, and increase risk of suicide. In fact, youth have the highest suicide rates of all inmates in jails. Youth are 19 times more likely to commit suicide in jail than youth in the general population and 36 times more likely to commit suicide in an adult jail than in a juvenile detention facility. Jail staff are simply not equipped to protect youth from the dangers of adult jails.

A Lack of Education and Training

Jails do not have the capacity to provide the necessary education and other programs crucial for the healthy development of adolescents. Even though legally required to, few jails provide appropriate education to youth. A BJS survey found that 40% of jails provided no educational services at all, only 11% of jails provided special education services, and only 7% provided vocational training. As many as one-half of all youth transferred to the adult system do not receive adult convictions, and are returned to the juvenile justice system or are not convicted at all. Many of these youth will have spent *at least one month* in an adult jail and one in five of these youth will have spent *over six months* in an adult jail. Without adequate education and other services, jails take youth off course.

Research conducted nationally by the MacArthur Foundation Research Network on Adolescent Development and Juvenile Justice, and other organizations, has also found that placing youth in the adult criminal justice system increases their likelihood of re-offending. Physicians and criminologists agree that children who are prosecuted in adult court are more likely to be rearrested more often and more quickly for serious offenses. The Centers for Disease Control and Prevention Task Force on Community Preventive Services released findings that show that transferring youth to the adult criminal system increases violence and concluded that policies that send youth to the adult criminal justice system, including placement of youth in adult jails, are "counterproductive for the purpose of reducing violence and enhancing public safety."

Finally, the federal Juvenile Justice and Delinquency Prevention Act (JJDPA) enacted over three decades ago was designed to keep youth out of jails. However, there is a loophole—the law does not protect youth prosecuted in the adult criminal system even though the original intent of the federal law was to remove youth from adult jails altogether. Congress should fix this problem by amending the JJDPA to protect all youth, no matter what court (juvenile or criminal) they are in, from being placed in an adult jail. Similarly, states and counties should update their state statutes and policies to prohibit the placement of youth in adult jails.

> "Boys sentenced to a correctional facility as juveniles were more likely to continue their offending during adulthood."

A Juvenile Justice System That Favors Incarceration Increases Crime

Dick Mendel

Incarcerating youth increases the risk that they will be involved in criminal activity, claims journalist Dick Mendel in the following viewpoint. In fact, the more youth are involved in the juvenile justice system, the more likely they will be arrested as adults, he asserts. Research suggests that once youth are arrested, they become labeled and treated as criminals, whether or not their behavior changes, Mendel maintains. Moreover, he argues, research shows that putting troubled youth together in a group tends to reinforce, not improve, bad behavior. Informal responses lead to better outcomes for troubled youth and for the community, he concludes.

As you read, consider the following questions:

1. According to Mendel, what percentage of French Canadian boys studied had adult criminal records by age twenty-five?

2. What does the author say is the impact of juvenile sanctions on young people's progress in school and success in the labor market?

3. What does the author claim happened to the number of youth adjudicated in juvenile courts from 1994 through 2005?

Is it time for the United States to haul in its law-and-order approach to adolescent misbehavior?

Time for principals to stop sending students to court for run-of-the-mill fistfights or mouthing off? For police to stop dragging kids to court over status offenses and disorderly conduct? For juvenile courts to stop imposing probation on youth wholesale, and for juvenile corrections systems to reduce their stubborn reliance on training schools?

Those are the unmistakable implications of an eye-opening Canadian study released in August [2009] that followed a group of disadvantaged Montreal boys throughout childhood and into adulthood. It found that—controlling for self-reported delinquency and a range of other variables—the more deeply involved a boy got with the juvenile justice system, the more likely he was to get arrested as an adult. Involvement with the juvenile system was the single-greatest predictor of criminality in the study—by far.

Exacerbating Delinquency

The study joins a stream of recent research indicating that, both here and abroad, juvenile justice systems are more likely to exacerbate delinquency than cure it, especially when young people are incarcerated or placed into group treatment programs where they interact with other troubled and troublemaking teens.

In the study, researchers began tracking more than 1,000 French Canadian kindergarten boys in 1984; all came from disadvantaged Montreal neighborhoods. The investigators evaluated the youths annually from ages 10 to 17, through interviews with parents, teachers, classmates and the young people themselves. They also searched court records to track the youths' contact with the justice system through age 25.

Among the 779 youths for whom complete data were compiled, nearly 15 percent had judicial records as juveniles and 18 percent had adult criminal records by age 25. Those with hyperactive/impulsive personalities or high levels of self-reported delinquency during adolescence were most likely to have adult records. Low family income, weak parental supervision and association with deviant peers were also correlated with adult crime.

Even controlling for those variables, the study found, youth who had been involved in juvenile court were seven times more likely to have adult criminal records than youth with the same backgrounds and self-reported delinquency but no juvenile court record. What's more, the study says, "The more restrictive and more intense the justice system intervention was, the greater was its negative impact."

Compared to youths with equivalent behavior and delinquency histories, but no history in juvenile court:

- Youths who received mild sentences (such as counseling, community service or restitution) were 2.3 times as likely to incur adult criminal records.

- Youths placed on probation were 14 times as likely to incur adult records.

- Youths placed in a juvenile correctional institution were 38 times as likely to have adult records.

"Placement in an institution," the study concludes, "exerts by far the strongest criminogenic effect."

Similar Conclusions Found Elsewhere

Shocking as these findings may seem, they confirm what criminologists have been finding for years: Juvenile court involvement typically leads to more, rather than less, criminality.

In 2007, a longitudinal study of Scottish youth ("Youth Justice? The Impact of System Contact on Patterns of Desistance from Offending") showed that those who faced a juvenile hearing were nearly twice as likely to admit engaging in serious offending (48 percent vs. 28 percent) in the following year as youth with identical backgrounds and prior self-reported offending behavior who did not face court hearings.

A 2003 study tracking youth in Denver and in Bremen, Germany ("The Effect of Juvenile Justice System Processing on Subsequent Delinquent and Criminal Behavior") found that, in both cities, "those arrested and sanctioned display higher frequencies of involvement in crime at later stages in their life than do their delinquent age mates who were not so sanctioned."

Likewise, a study tracking several thousand Philadelphia children born in 1958 found that boys sentenced to a correctional facility as juveniles were more likely to continue their offending during adulthood than similar youth who were not incarcerated.

Looking for Causes

While the recent Montreal study did not tease out the reasons why juvenile court involvement led to worse outcomes, prior research suggests three causes:

1. "Labeling"—The idea is that once youth get arrested and go to court, school officials, police, courts and corrections systems treat them more severely and entrap them in the justice system. For instance, the recent Scottish study found that

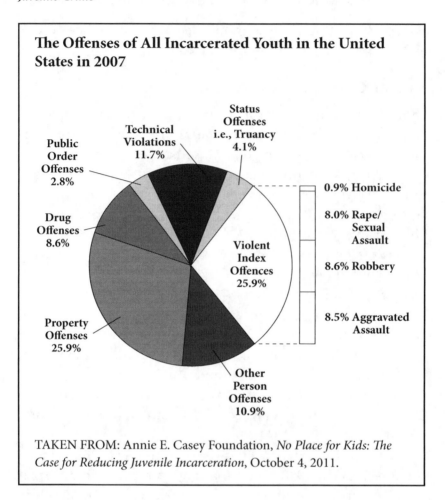

The Offenses of All Incarcerated Youth in the United States in 2007

Public Order Offenses 2.8%

Technical Violations 11.7%

Status Offenses i.e., Truancy 4.1%

Drug Offenses 8.6%

Violent Index Offences 25.9%

0.9% Homicide

8.0% Rape/ Sexual Assault

8.6% Robbery

8.5% Aggravated Assault

Property Offenses 25.9%

Other Person Offenses 10.9%

TAKEN FROM: Annie E. Casey Foundation, *No Place for Kids: The Case for Reducing Juvenile Incarceration*, October 4, 2011.

"certain groups of youngsters—who might readily be termed the 'usual suspects'—become the principal focus of agency attention. These youngsters are recycled into the hearing system again and again, no matter whether their offending has diminished in seriousness or frequency, or whether their formally assessed levels of need have been addressed."

In turn, this increased contact with the system reduces the chances that the youth will desist from delinquency.

A California study in the 1980s randomly assigned youth who committed delinquent offenses to either outright release, referral to counseling, placement in counseling or prosecution in juvenile court. In follow-up surveys, youth from all groups reported similar levels of subsequent misbehavior, but youth released outright proved far less likely to be taken to court and sanctioned for future offenses than youth in any of the other groups. The stronger the initial sanction, the more likely the youth would be rearrested and adjudicated in juvenile court.

2. The impact of juvenile sanctions on young people's progress in school and subsequent success in the labor market—According to a U.S. Department of Education study (cited in *The Dangers of Detention: The Impact of Incarcerating Youth in Detention and Other Secure Facilities*), three-fifths of youth incarcerated as ninth graders either never re-enrolled in school or dropped out within five months of returning to school.

Bruce Western of Princeton University has found that people in their early 20s who had been locked up as juveniles worked three weeks less per year than equivalent young adults who were not incarcerated. Even after 15 years, those incarcerated as juveniles were working significantly less than their counterparts who were never sentenced to a youth corrections facility.

This damage to youths' progress in education and employment is especially important given what we know about the nature of delinquency: that a large majority of youth commit delinquent acts during adolescence, and about one-third commit serious crimes. Yet most youth grow out of delinquency as they assume adult roles in society.

"What if our traditional juvenile justice practices interrupted this normal trajectory and, instead of impeding future delinquency, actually caused harm to our communities by increasing offending?" asks Barry Holman, who oversees research and quality assurance for the Department of Youth Rehabilitation Services in Washington, D.C., and has served as director of research and public policy for the National Center on Institutions and Alternatives.

3. "Deviant peer contagion"—This is sociologists' fancy label for the simple idea that if you throw a lot of troubled teenagers together in a group, they're likely to reinforce each others' negative conduct and behave worse. This dynamic is most apparent in the rueful results of the country's training schools and other juvenile correctional facilities, which routinely show recidivism rates of 50 percent to 80 percent.

Longitudinal studies about the impact of juvenile incarceration yield results ranging from bad to worse. The most favorable, like the initial report of the MacArthur Foundation's "Pathways to Desistance" project released in December, find that despite the enormous expense of incarceration, youth sentenced to juvenile facilities are no less likely to re-offend than youth supervised in the community at a fraction of the cost. Other research, like the new Montreal study, find that juvenile incarceration substantially increases future offending.

Barry Feld, a leading juvenile justice scholar at the University of Minnesota, has called juvenile training schools and youth prisons "the one extensively evaluated and clearly ineffective method to 'treat' delinquents."

Even when youth aren't locked up together in institutions, group treatment can have negative and even counterproductive results. Richard Tremblay, one of the Montreal study's authors, believes this negative peer dynamic is probably the biggest culprit behind the juvenile justice system's poor outcomes in Montreal and elsewhere. "By putting adolescents together you're only encouraging them to imitate each other," he says. "Most of these kids are receiving a treatment that is seriously harming them. . . . And it's costly."

The Hard Line Continues

How are juvenile court and corrections officials responding to the evidence that the deeper youth are involved in the juvenile courts and the more correctional "treatment" they receive, the worse their results?

For the most part they're not. Notwithstanding some high-profile reform efforts like the Annie E. Casey Foundation's 100-site detention reform initiative, most juvenile justice systems have instead been expanding their nets rather than limiting formal court processing and reducing reliance on correctional sanctions and treatment, as the research suggests.

From 1994 through 2005, a period when youth homicides and other serious juvenile crimes declined dramatically, the number of youth adjudicated in juvenile courts increased sharply for virtually every class of minor offense: liquor law adjudications up 57 percent, adjudication for "public order offenses" up 70 percent, simple assault adjudications (typically fighting) up 80 percent, and adjudications for "disorderly conduct" up 109 percent. . . .

Veteran juvenile justice researcher Jeffrey Butts takes a harsh view of the juvenile system's intransigence. "If you're going to take away a kid's liberty or impose some sanction on him," he says, "you ought to make damned sure that what you're doing does more good than harm."

"Most states that have downsized or closed [juvenile] facilities have been able to save or reallocate money while protecting public safety."

Efforts to Reduce Juvenile Incarceration Have Led to Positive Outcomes

National Juvenile Justice Network

In the following viewpoint, the National Juvenile Justice Network (NJJN) argues that state programs designed to decrease the number of youth in juvenile facilities have cut costs and increased public safety. In fact, California saved over $525 million between 2007 and 2010 by cutting the number of incarcerated youth. Rather than automatically placing troubled youth in juvenile facilities, whether or not they pose a risk to public safety, states should place them in programs that meet their needs, the author asserts. Indeed, NJJN claims, removing youths from their families should be a last resort. The National Juvenile Justice Network works with state juvenile justice coalitions and organizations to promote fair, equitable, and developmentally appropriate juvenile justice policies.

As you read, consider the following questions:

1. According to NJJN, what are some of the reasons states are closing juvenile facilities?

2. What does NJJN mean when it warns that states should be careful not to "squeeze the balloon"?

3. Where are the highest rates of disproportionate minority contact seen in the juvenile justice system, in the author's view?

Over the past several years, many states across the country have dramatically reduced the number of youth held in secure facilities. Some states have achieved these reductions by downsizing existing populations in secure facilities; others have shuttered entire institutions. While the population reduction is noteworthy in and of itself, it has been accompanied by powerful data. Most states that have downsized or closed facilities have been able to save or reallocate money while protecting public safety, due to the high expense of incarceration, and the greater effectiveness of less costly community-based alternatives. Additionally, evidence shows that these population reductions have not, as some may have predicted, led to an increase in youth crime; in fact, crime rates have either remained steady or even declined, demonstrating an increase in public safety. The simultaneous increase in public safety and reduction of secure facility populations is supported by research indicating that community-based supervision is as effective as incarceration for youth who have committed serious offenses.

Downsizing Done Right

This [viewpoint] includes examples of states that have reduced their juvenile facility populations and are now not only reaping the rewards of newfound funds that can be redirected into more effective community-based services for youth, but also seeing a better return on their investment in terms of juvenile rehabilitation and public safety. These positive changes are the result of many factors. Some closures have been mandated by legislatures, while others are the result of reform-minded administrators who acknowledge more appropriate and effective ways to respond to court-involved youth. Other closures have resulted from lawsuits that have exposed horrific conditions in facilities and regular abuse. In almost all cases, however, these changes represent years of dedicated work from local advocacy organizations, often in partnership with private foundations and government stakeholders. . . .

The trend toward facility closures and the reduction in the number of youth in secure confinement is promising. States can achieve the best results for budgets, public safety, and youth by considering the factors below as they downsize juvenile facility populations.

Treat youth appropriately. Downsizing is an opportunity to utilize and develop programming that is the most effective for youth and public safety and financially sensible for states and communities. The adult criminal system is not designed for youth in conflict with the law, and it is not adequately equipped to serve such youth successfully. Many states are recognizing that youth must be treated as youth, and should be retained in a juvenile system that is designed specifically for their needs. Likewise, while youth may well benefit from mental health services, not all youth who come into conflict with the law need the in-depth treatment provided by residential mental health programs. States should be careful not to "squeeze the balloon" and simply shuffle youth from juvenile facilities into adult prisons, mental health facilities, or other institutions. Additionally, as the population of youth incarcerated in juvenile facilities declines, states should consider opportunities to more effectively serve juvenile offenders who are confined in adult facilities by transferring them back to the safer and more developmentally appropriate juvenile system.

Success in California

California is notorious for the number of people incarcerated by the state, and in the past, youth were certainly no exception. However, recent years have brought litigation around dangerous conditions in the facilities, which has resulted in media attention, stakeholder education about the problematic conditions, advocacy by a broad spectrum of organizations . . . , and increased costs to the state for the confinement of youth. These developments have led to higher numbers of youth being treated by community-based programs in some counties, legislation restricting the types of offenses that can lead to state imprisonment, and budget realignment that redirects funds from state juvenile justice to the counties. These practice and policy changes . . . have contributed to a dramatic drop in the population sent to California's state youth facilities over the past fifteen years.

The Facts:

- The population of California's youth prisons has declined from a staggering 10,122 in 1996 to 1,254 at the end of 2010, a nearly 88 percent decrease.

- At a rate of $218,000 per year per youth in 2007, California avoided spending over $525 million on incarceration between 2007 and 2010. . . .

- From 1996 to 2009, both felony and misdemeanor arrest rates for juveniles steadily declined to their 25-year lows.

- Juvenile felony arrests have declined from 2,902 in 1991 to 1,290 in 2009, a 50-year low.

"Bringing Youth Home: A National Movement to Increase Public Safety, Rehabilitate Youth and Save Money," National Juvenile Justice Network, July 2011. pp. 2–3.

Reevaluate which youth are being incarcerated. Many states default to incarcerating youth who have committed crimes. Secure facility population reductions give states the opportunity to be thoughtful and deliberate in their decisions to lock up youth. States should use a validated risk-assessment tool to evaluate whether or not a youth is truly a threat to public safety and should be incarcerated. Likewise, states should assess the needs of each youth and thereby determine an appropriate disposition that involves programming specifically tailored to each youth. Lastly, states should consider whether the infraction committed by a youth truly warrants incarceration; many states incarcerate large numbers of youth who have committed relatively minor offenses and whose chances for rehabilitation are much greater in a community-based program. The removal of a youth from his or her family and placement in a secure facility should always be the disposition of last resort, and for the shortest time possible.

Stay focused on disproportionate minority contact. Nationally, African American and Latino youth are overrepresented at every point in the juvenile justice system and are transferred to the adult system at rates disproportionate to those of white youth. This disproportionate minority contact (DMC) with the juvenile and criminal justice systems increases as youth move deeper into the system; the highest rates of disproportionality are seen in commitments to juvenile residential placements and incarceration in adult prisons. Downsizing secure facility populations presents a unique opportunity to look at DMC from a different angle: Rather than only focusing on youth who enter the system, states can carefully evaluate which youth are released from facilities, and ensure equitable treatment of all youth. The policies and practices that lead to facility closures or downsizing should be, at a minimum, neutral with regard to race and ethnicity, and ideally targeted at reducing disproportionality in confinement. Additionally, as with all aspects of the juvenile justice system, states should ensure careful data collection on downsizing and facility closures as a means to evaluate DMC and planned reforms, and to develop further solutions as needed.

Ensure accountability. Some states that have closed state-run facilities have instead contracted with private companies to run institutions or residential treatment centers for youth. Some private companies run excellent programs for youth. However, accountability is an issue with all privately run programs and facilities, and private companies may prioritize profits over the safe care and well-being of youth. When a state enters into a contract with a private company, there must be a clear plan for both internal and external oversight in order to ensure proper protections for youth and their families. States must also scrutinize any claims by private companies that they offer a less expensive option for youth, to ensure that claimed expenses account for contract oversight costs, transportation costs, general overhead costs, and other expenses that are spread across agencies (such as education and health care costs).

Keep youth in homelike settings. Facility shutdowns should lead to expanded use of local, community-based programs, which are usually much less expensive, and more effective, than traditional secure confinement. If youth must be removed from their communities, they should be placed in small facilities with homelike characteristics, in close proximity to their home communities. The closure of secure facilities presents an opportunity to get youth out of larger, prison-like institutions and to avoid the numerous, proven ill effects of institutionalization. When deciding which facilities to close, states should ensure that youth are not transferred to a more secure environment due to the closure of a lower-security facility, but rather are moved into the least restrictive, most homelike environment possible.

Redirect funds to alternatives to confinement. States can save significant funds by shuttering juvenile institutions. The

American Correctional Association estimates that it costs nearly $88,000 per year ($240.99 per day) on average for each youth in a residential juvenile facility, and some states report costs as high as $726 per day (nearly $265,000 per year) for a juvenile residential bed. Additionally, states may find that as youth are moved out of secure facilities and into less restrictive programs that target their underlying needs, additional federal funding through Medicaid and Title IV-E [federal funding to states for foster children] might become available. In light of the high costs of incarceration and the current fiscal climate, many governors, legislators, and administrators are planning or considering facility closures. As states move toward downsizing and facility closures, they should consider the best ways to reinvest at least a portion of the cost savings into community-based programs for youth in conflict with the law. Such investments will ensure that youth are adequately supported by proven programming, which in turn will help truly rehabilitate youth and reduce recidivism, thereby increasing public safety and saving money in the long term.

States can also consider legislatively enacting a fiscal realignment plan to reduce incarceration costs for the state, while incentivizing counties to develop effective community-based alternatives to incarceration. In such models, states offer financial incentives to counties that keep youth out of state institutions and instead treat youth locally. Wisconsin, California, Illinois, and Ohio have had much success with fiscal realignment models, and several other states are currently considering such legislation.

Incarceration as a Last Resort

Due to the squeeze of shrunken budgets, there is more reason than ever to reduce the number of incarcerated youth. Ample evidence from many states shows that such population reductions do not have negative consequences, but instead serve as a means to reduce spending while treating youth in a more appropriate and effective way. As states search for ways to plug fiscal holes, they should consider the economic and social benefits of using incarceration only as a last resort and for the shortest time possible. States should first look to serve youth in conflict with the law through proven, cost-effective, community-based programming.

"Life without parole (LWOP) is, for certain types of juvenile offenders, an effective, appropriate, and lawful punishment."

It Should Be Possible to Sentence Juveniles to Life Without Parole

Charles D. Stimson and Andrew M. Grossman

Forty-three state legislatures have set the maximum punishment of juveniles to life without parole (LWOP), maintain Charles D. Stimson and Andrew M. Grossman in the following viewpoint. This reflects a national consensus that LWOP is an appropriate punishment for violent juvenile criminals, they claim. Nevertheless, opponents use misinformation and misleading tactics to persuade policy makers to abolish LWOP for violent juveniles. For example, Stimson and Grossman argue, anti-LWOP advocates describe these juveniles as innocents when in fact they are remorseless killers. LWOP is a rare but reasonable sentence for violent juvenile crimes, they conclude. Stimson and Grossman are legal policy analysts for the Heritage Foundation, a conservative think tank.

Charles D. Stimson and Andrew M. Grossman, "Adult Time for Adult Crimes: Life Without Parole for Juvenile Killers and Violent Teens," Heritage Foundation, August 2009. www.heritage.org. Copyright © 2009 The Heritage Foundation. All rights reserved. Reproduced by permission.

As you read, consider the following questions:

1. How many juveniles were arrested for murder in the United States between 1980 and 2005, according to Stimson and Grossman?

2. In the authors' opinion, what language do LWOP opponents use to gain sympathy for their views?

3. How did the judge's account of the facts differ from the picture of Ashley Jones painted by LWOP opponents, in the authors' view?

The United States leads the Western world in juvenile crime and has done so for decades. Juveniles commit murder, rape, robbery, aggravated assault, and other serious crimes—particularly violent crimes—in numbers that dwarf those of America's international peers.

The plain statistics are shocking. Between 1980 and 2005, 43,621 juveniles were arrested for murder in the United States. The picture is just as bleak with respect to arrests for rape (109,563), robbery (818,278), and aggravated assault (1,240,199).

Commonsense Measures

In response to this flood of juvenile offenders, state legislatures have enacted commonsense measures to protect their citizens and hold these dangerous criminals accountable. The states spend billions of dollars each year on their juvenile justice systems, which handle the vast majority of juvenile offenders. Most states have also enacted laws that allow particularly violent and mature juveniles to be tried as adults. And for the very worst juvenile offenders, 43 state legislatures and the federal government have set the maximum punishment at life without the possibility of parole.

This represents an overwhelming national consensus that life without parole (LWOP) is, for certain types of juvenile offenders, an effective, appropriate, and lawful punishment. Moreover, no state court that has addressed the constitutionality of sentencing juvenile offenders to life without parole has struck the sentence down as unconstitutional. Federal courts have consistently reached the same conclusion. . . .

A Small but Coordinated Movement

Opponents of tough sentences for serious juvenile offenders have been working for years to abolish the sentence of life without the possibility of parole. Though representing relatively few, these groups are highly organized, well funded, and passionate about their cause. Emboldened by the Supreme Court's decision in *Roper* [referring to *Roper v. Simmons*, 2005], which relied on the "cruel and unusual punishments" language of the Eighth Amendment to the Constitution to prohibit capital sentences for juveniles, they have set about to extend the result of *Roper* to life without parole.

These groups wrap their reports and other products in the language of *Roper* and employ sympathetic terms like "child" and "children" and *Roper*-like language such as "death sentence" instead of the actual sentence of life without parole. Their reports are adorned with pictures of children, most of whom appear to be five to eight years old, despite the fact that the youngest person serving life without parole in the United States is 14 years old and most are 17 or 18 years old.

A Campaign of Misinformation

A careful reading of these groups' report articles and press releases reveals that their messages and themes have been tightly coordinated. There is a very unsubtle similarity in terminology among organizations in characterizing the sentence of life without parole for juvenile offenders. For example, they consistently decline to label teenage offenders "juveniles" despite the fact that the term is used by the states, lawyers, prosecutors, state statutes, judges, parole officers, and everyone else in the juvenile justice system. Instead, they use "child."

There is nothing wrong, of course, with advocacy groups coordinating their language and message. The problem is that this important public policy debate has been shaped by a carefully crafted campaign of misinformation.

The issue of juvenile offenders and the proper sentence they are due is much too important to be driven by manufactured statistics, a misreading of a Supreme Court case, and fallacious assertions that the United States is in violation of international law. Instead, the debate should be based on real facts and statistics, a proper reading of precedent, an intelligent understanding of federal and state sovereignty, and a proper understanding of our actual international obligations.

A One-Sided Debate

Regrettably, that has not been the case, as opponents of life without parole for juvenile offenders have monopolized the debate. As a result, legislatures, courts, the media, and the public have been misled on crucial points.

One prominent example is a frequently cited statistic on the number of juvenile offenders currently serving life-without-parole sentences. Nearly all reports published on the subject and dozens of newscasts and articles based on those reports state that there are at least 2,225 juveniles sentenced to life without parole. That number first appeared in a 2005 report by Amnesty International and Human Rights Watch, "The Rest of Their Lives: Life Without Parole for Child Offenders in the United States."

But a careful look at the data and consultation with primary sources—that is, state criminal-justice officials—reveals that this statistic is seriously flawed. . . . Officials in some states reject as incorrect the figures assigned to their states.

Crime in the United States Compared to Other Nations

- In 1998 alone, 24,537,600 recorded crimes were committed in the United States.

- Of the 72 countries that reported recorded crimes to the United Nations' seventh survey of crime trends, the United States ranked first in total recorded crimes.

- Worse still, the United States reported more crimes than the next six countries (Germany, England/Wales, France, South Africa, Russia, and Canada) combined. Their total was 23,111,318.

- Even more tellingly, the U.S. had a higher crime rate than all of those countries, except for England, which experienced disproportionate rates of property crimes but much lower rates of violent crimes.

Charles D. Stimson and Andrew M. Grossman,
"Adult Time for Adult Crimes: Life Without
Parole for Juvenile Killers and Violent Teens,"
Heritage Foundation, August 2009, p. 21.

Others admit that they have no way of knowing how many juvenile offenders in their states have been sentenced to life without parole—and that, by extension, neither could activist groups.

Nonetheless, this statistic has gone unchallenged even as it has been cited in appellate briefs and oral arguments before state supreme courts and even in a petition to the United States Supreme Court. All of these courts have been asked to make public policy based on factual representations that even cursory research would demonstrate are questionable.

An Unrealistic Portrait

Another example is the unrealistic portrait of the juvenile offenders who are sentenced to life without parole that activist groups have painted. Nearly every report contains sympathetic summaries of juvenile offenders' cases that gloss over the real facts of the crimes, deploying lawyerly language and euphemism to disguise brutality and violence.

For example, consider the case of Ashley Jones. The Equal Justice Initiative's 2007 report describes Ms. Jones's offense as follows: "At 14, Ashley tried to escape the violence and abuse by running away with an older boyfriend who shot and killed her grandfather and aunt. Her grandmother and sister, who were injured during the offense, want Ashley to come home."

The judge's account of the facts, however, presents a somewhat different picture. An excerpt:

> When Ashley realized her aunt was still breathing, she hit her in the head with a heater, stabbed her in the chest and attempted to set her room on fire. . . .

> As ten-year-old Mary Jones [Ashley's sister] attempted to run, Ashley grabbed her and began hitting her. [Ashley's boyfriend] put the gun in young Mary's face and told her that that was how she would die. Ashley intervened and said, "No, let me do it," and proceeded to stab her little sister fourteen times.

In a similar vein, many of the studies feature pictures of children who are far younger than any person actually serving life without parole in the United States. When these reports do include an actual picture of a juvenile offender, the picture is often one taken years before the crime was committed. The public could be forgiven for believing incorrectly that children under 14 are regularly sentenced to life behind bars without the possibility of release.

Abusing Judicial Precedent

A final example is the legality of life-without-parole sentences for juvenile offenders. Opponents make the claim, among many others, that these sentences violate the United States' obligations under international law. Yet they usually fail to mention that no court has endorsed this view, and rarely do they explain the implications of the fact that the United States has not ratified the treaty that they most often cite, the Convention on the Rights of the Child, and has carved out legal exceptions (called "reservations") to others.

Further, they often abuse judicial precedent by improperly extending the death penalty–specific logic and language of *Roper* into the non–death penalty arena, an approach that the Supreme Court has repeatedly rejected. Again, the public could be forgiven for believing incorrectly that the Supreme Court, particularly in *Roper*, has all but declared the imposition of life sentences without parole for juvenile offenders to be unconstitutional. A more honest reading of the precedent, however, compels the opposite conclusion: that the sentence is not constitutionally suspect.

The Whole Story

Public policy should be based on facts, not false statistics and misleading legal claims. For that reason, we undertook the research to identify those states that have authorized life without parole for juvenile offenders and wrote to every major district attorney's office across those 43 states. To understand how prosecutors are using life-without-parole sentences and the types of crimes and criminals for which such sentences are imposed, we asked each office for case digests of juvenile offenders who were prosecuted by their offices and received the specific sentence of life without parole.

The response from prosecutors around the country was overwhelming. Prosecutors from across the United States sent us case digests, including official court documents, police reports, judges' findings, photos of the defendants and victims, motions, newspaper articles, and more. . . . In sharp contrast to the practices of other reports, these case studies recount all of the relevant facts of the crimes, as found by a jury or judge and recorded in official records (which are cited), in neutral language. . . .

A Reasonable Policy

Based on this research, we conclude that the sentence of life without parole for juvenile offenders is reasonable, constitutional, and (appropriately) rare. Our survey of the cases shows that some juveniles commit horrific crimes with full knowledge of their actions and intent to bring about the results. In constitutional terms, the Supreme Court's own jurisprudence, including *Roper*, draws a clear line between the sentence of death and all others, including life without parole; further, to reach its result, *Roper* actually depends on the availability of life without parole for juvenile offenders. We also find that while most states allow life-without-parole sentences for juvenile offenders, judges generally have broad discretion in sentencing, and most juvenile offenders do not receive that sentence.

We conclude, then, that reports by activist groups on life without parole for juvenile offenders are at best misleading and in some instances simply wrong in their facts, analyses, conclusions, and recommendations. Regrettably, the claims made by these groups have been repeated so frequently that lawmakers, judges, the media, and the public risk losing sight of their significant bias.

To foster informed debate, more facts—particularly, good state-level statistics—are needed about the use of life-without-parole sentences for juvenile offenders. But even on the basis of current data, as insufficient as they are, legislators should take note of how these sentences are actually applied and reject any attempts to repeal life-without-parole sentences for juvenile offenders.

> *"Sentencing youth to life without parole strips our young people of hope and the opportunity for rehabilitation."*

Juveniles Should Not Be Sentenced to Life Without Parole

Linda L. White

In the following viewpoint, Linda L. White, the mother of a victim raped and murdered by two fifteen-year-old boys, argues that sentencing juveniles to life without the possibility of parole ignores that youth are different from adults and does not allow for the possibility of rehabilitation. Although many believe that criminals should suffer, she claims in this testimony before a subcommittee of the US House of Representatives that punishment does little to change behavior. Moreover, White maintains, one of the boys who killed her daughter suffered abuse at home and in foster care, and he tried to commit suicide several times as a young boy. When she met him, he expressed his remorse, confirming her belief in restorative justice.

Linda L. White, "Testimony of Linda L. White," Judiciary Committee of the US House of Representatives, June 9, 2009. http://judiciary.house.gov.

As you read, consider the following questions:

1. What does White claim was the most rewarding work she has ever done?

2. What does the author claim was different about her journey to healing than what she often sees in victim/survivors?

3. When did the non-personhood of the killers of the author's daughter change?

Thank you for inviting me to discuss the issue of juvenile life without possibility of parole, and specifically H.R. 2289, the Juvenile Justice Accountability and Improvement Act of 2009.[1] My name is Linda White and ... I am a member of Murder Victims' Families for Reconciliation. I live near Houston, Texas, where I have resided for 35 years. I am here to support the bill before you because it allows for periodic reviews of life without parole sentences given to juveniles.

A Life-Changing Event

Until November of 1986, I was not very knowledgeable or very interested, to be quite frank, in criminal justice matters in general, and certainly not juvenile justice matters. That changed quite suddenly and dramatically late that November when our 26-year-old daughter, Cathy, went missing for five days and was then found dead following a sexual assault by two 15-year-old boys. I spent the better part of a year in limbo awaiting their trials, as they had both been certified to stand trial as adults.

During that time, the only information I had on either of them was that they both had long juvenile records. There was

---

1. While the Juvenile Justice Accountability and Improvement Act of 2009 never became law, on May 17, 2010, the Supreme Court decided in *Graham v. Florida* that juveniles may not be sentenced to life in prison without parole for any crime short of homicide.

never any doubt about their guilt, as they had confessed to the rape and murder and lead the police to her body after they had been detained by the police in another city in Texas. The court-appointed attorneys for both pled them out and they were sentenced to long prison terms with no chance at parole for at least eighteen years. They came up for parole in 2004 and were both given five-year setoffs, so they remain in prison at this time. I assume they will come up again later on this year.

Becoming Educated

The year after my daughter was murdered, I returned to college to become a death educator and grief counselor. Since that time, I have received a bachelor's degree in psychology, a master's degree in clinical psychology, and a doctorate in educational human resource development with a focus in adult education. I fell in love with teaching along the way and never got my professional counseling credentials, but I have counseled informally through church and my teaching. During the time I taught at the university level, I taught upper-level college courses for eight-and-a-half years in prison, the most rewarding work I have ever done, and the most healing for me as the mother of a murder victim.

In addition to the formal schooling I've had, I have also educated myself in the area of criminal justice. I heard a lot of information when I attended victims' groups and I wanted to know if it was accurate. I have found out that, for the most part, it was not. One notable example: Texas prisons are about as far as you can get from country clubs. Many of our citizens, and certainly victims of crime, want the men and women who are convicted of criminal activity to suffer as much as possible in prison, believing that this is the way they will turn from a life of crime. I no longer believe this to be true, and I have become a devout believer in restorative justice as opposed to retributive justice. It does not mean that I think in-

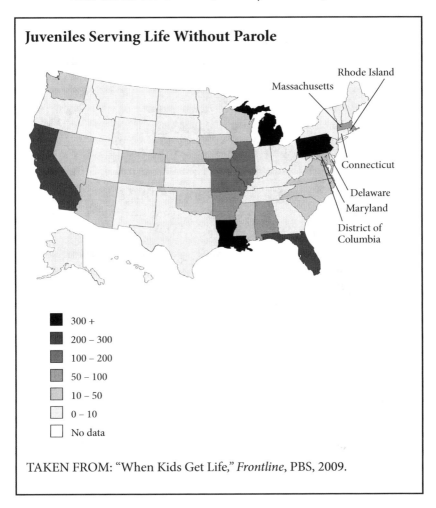

Juveniles Serving Life Without Parole

Rhode Island

Massachusetts

Connecticut

Delaware

Maryland

District of Columbia

- 300 +
- 200 – 300
- 100 – 200
- 50 – 100
- 10 – 50
- 0 – 10
- No data

TAKEN FROM: "When Kids Get Life," *Frontline*, PBS, 2009.

carceration is always wrong, but neither do I believe that it should be our first inclination, for juveniles or for adults. And neither am I a great believer in long sentences, for most offenders. As a psychology student and teacher, I have learned that punishment is the least effective means to change behavior, and that it often has negative side effects as well.

The Journey to Healing

My journey to healing after my daughter's murder was different than what I often see in victim/survivors, for I had concentrated on healing for my family and me, and because I focused on education over the years. At first it was education about grief and how to help my young granddaughter with hers, and then, when I returned to college, it became about psychology and issues related to death and dying. Eventually, it became concentrated in criminal justice. Early on, I saw much that was violent in our system perhaps necessarily so at times—but still, it seemed to me that we returned violence for violence in so many ways. I kept my mind and heart open to another means of doing justice, one that would be based on nonviolent ideals and means. Restorative justice is that paradigm and I have become one of its greatest proponents. That is what actually led me to seek a mediated conversation with either of the young men who killed my Cathy.

As I said previously, for many years, I only knew that the boys who killed my daughter were juveniles with long criminal records. In 2000, I found out that one of them, Gary Brown, was willing to meet with me in a mediated dialogue as part of a program that we have in our Texas Department of Criminal Justice's victims' services division. He was apparently very remorseful by that time and had prayed for a chance to tell us that. During the next year, Gary, with the help of our mediator Ellen Halbert, and my daughter Ami (Cathy's daughter whom we had raised and adopted) and I did a great deal of reflective work to prepare for our meeting. During that time, I found out from Gary's records that his long juvenile record began at the age of eight with his running away from abusive situations, both at home and in foster care eventually. If I were being abused emotionally, physically, and sexually, I think I'd run away, too; it seems quite rational to me. I also found out that his first suicide attempt was at the age of eight, the first of ten attempts. I have a grandson just about that age right now, and it breaks my heart to think of a child like that trying to take his own life because it is so miserable.

Recognizing a Killer's Humanity

Until the time that I met with Gary, I had never laid eyes on him and had, over the years, gradually come to ignore his existence. Both the offenders became non-persons to me, in effect. Once I knew that Gary wanted to meet me, that non-personhood totally changed for me; he became as human to me as the men I had taught in prison. That in and of itself was a relief, I think, since part of me revolted at the idea of forgetting him in any way at all. As the time approached for us to meet, I know that my daughter and Gary both became more and more apprehensive, but not me. I couldn't wait to see him and tell him how much I believed in his remorse and was grateful for it. I know that this unusual response to the killer of one's beloved child was only possible through my discovery of restorative justice and, of course, by the grace of God. I strongly believe that most of my journey over the last 22 years had been through grace. Otherwise, I have no explanation for it.

My meeting with him was everything I expected and more. Since it was made into a documentary, I have been privileged to have it shown around the world for training and educational purposes, and I have heard from many who have seen it and felt blessed by the experience. I am sometimes invited to go with the film to answer questions and reflect on my experience. I also go into prison, especially with a victim/offender encounter program we have in Texas called Bridges to Life, a faith-based restorative justice curriculum, where my film is used to educate offenders related to victim empathy. I have been deeply blessed by this work and I feel Cathy's presence in it every time I stand before a group either in or out of prison and reflect on my journey.

A Responsibility to Youth

My education and years of teaching developmental psychology have taught me that young people are just different qualitatively from the adults we hope they become. And my experience with Gary has taught me that we have a responsibility to protect our youth from the kind of childhood that he had, and from treatment that recklessly disregards their inherent vulnerability as children. Sentencing youth to life without parole strips our young people of hope and the opportunity for rehabilitation. It ignores what science tells us: that youth are fundamentally different from adults both physically and emotionally. Even given the trauma, and incredible loss my family experienced, I still believe that young people need to be held accountable in a way that reflects their ability to grow and change. Gary is proof that young people, even those who have done horrible things, can be reformed.

> "Research . . . suggests that minority youth receive harsher treatment than their white counterparts at nearly every stage of the juvenile justice process."

The Juvenile Justice System Should Address Racial Inequalities

Jeff Armour and Sarah Hammond

In the following viewpoint, Jeff Armour and Sarah Hammond maintain that minorities make up a majority of the youth in the juvenile justice system and receive harsher treatment than whites. Research suggests that one explanation is that minorities often live in urban areas where sentences are usually harsher. Other research points to police practices that target low-income neighborhoods where minorities are often concentrated, Armour and Hammond claim. According to the authors, policies that eliminate police responses that unnecessarily involve minority youth and that support community-based programs rather than deten-

tion have proven successful at reducing racial inequalities in the juvenile justice system. Armour and Hammond conduct research for the National Conference of State Legislatures' criminal justice program.

As you read, consider the following questions:

1. What did the 2003 National Survey on Drug Use and Health find was true of both minority and white youth?

2. According to Armour and Hammond, what federal law directed states to address racial disparities in their juvenile justice systems?

3. Why is data collection a common problem when studying minority contact reduction policies, in the authors' view?

Minority youth are disproportionately represented throughout juvenile justice systems in nearly every state in the nation. Disproportionate minority contact in juvenile justice occurs when minority youth come into contact with the system at a higher rate than their white counterparts. African Americans, Hispanics, Asians, Pacific Islanders and Native Americans comprise a combined one-third of the nation's youth population. Yet they account for over two-thirds of the youth in secure juvenile facilities.

Research by the National Council on Crime and Delinquency and the Center for Children's Law and Policy suggests that minority youth receive harsher treatment than their white counterparts at nearly every stage of the juvenile justice process. Minority juveniles are confined and sentenced for longer periods and are less likely to receive alternative sentences or probation compared to white juveniles.

Various explanations have emerged for the disproportionate treatment of minorities. They range from jurisdictional issues, certain police practices and punitive juvenile crime legislation of the 1990s to perceived racial bias in the system.

A Jurisdictional Explanation

The Office of Juvenile Justice and Delinquency Prevention (OJJDP) points out that results can depend on the jurisdiction in which the youth is processed. Cases adjudicated in urban areas, for example, are more likely to result in harsher results than similar cases adjudicated in nonurban areas. Because minority populations are concentrated in urban areas, a geographic effect may work to over-represent minorities statewide.

Another contributing factor related to urbanization is the location and visibility of minority youth crimes. According to the OJJDP, although white youth tend to use and sell drugs in their homes, minority youth are more likely to do so on street corners or in public neighborhood gathering spots.

Law Enforcement Practices

Police practices that target low-income urban neighborhoods and use group arrest procedures also can contribute to disproportionate minority contact. OJJDP arrest rate statistics illustrate that African American youth are arrested at much higher rates than their white peers for drug, property and violent crimes. [John D. and Catherine T.] MacArthur Foundation research shows African American youth are arrested at twice the rate of their white peers for drug crimes. Although these statistics suggest that minority youth simply commit more crimes, the matter is more complicated. A 2003 National Survey on Drug Use and Health by the Substance Abuse and Mental Health Services Administration documented that white youth are just as likely—or even more so—to be involved with illegal drug use and sales.

Punitive Juvenile Laws

In the early 1990s, states reacted to a spike in juvenile homicides with handguns by enacting tough laws that made it easier to try and sentence youth as adults. Many states enacted "automatic transfer laws" to exempt certain crimes from juvenile court jurisdiction. Under these laws, a juvenile is automatically referred to adult court for adjudication based on the alleged crime. The legislation also provided prosecutors and judges with more discretion to try juveniles as adults.

Research indicates that automatic transfer provisions have disproportionately affected minority youth. OJJDP's data show that African American and Native American youth are more likely to face conviction in adult court, especially for drug-related crimes. Analysis by the National Council on Crime and Delinquency indicates that three out of four of the 4,100 new admissions to adult prisons were minority youth. Another study completed in 2005 by Building Blocks for Youth showed that 85 percent of youth transferred to adult court under Illinois' automatic transfer law were African American.

Racial Bias

Racial bias within the justice system also is cited as a reason for over-representation of minority youth. OJJDP's analysis of various studies spanning 12 years reveals that, in approximately two-thirds of the studies, "negative race effects" (meaning race explains why minorities remain in the system) were present at various stages of the juvenile justice process.

The complex explanations for disproportionate minority contact along with sensitive race and ethnicity issues make it an important and difficult challenge for states.

Federal Solutions

The federal Juvenile Justice and Delinquency Prevention Act [JJDPA] of 1974 directed states to recognize and address racial disparities in their juvenile justice systems. Amendments to the act have since broadened its scope from "disproportionate minority confinement" to "disproportionate minority contact" related to all stages of discretion and dealing with youth in the juvenile justice process. Under existing law, states are re-

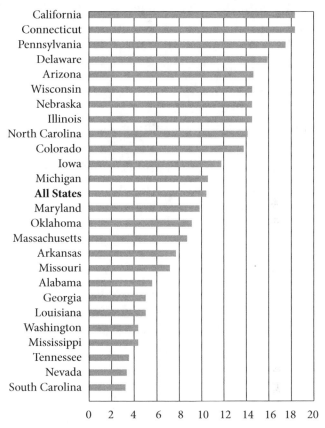

Ratio of Black to White Youth Serving Life Without Parole Sentences

Number of black youths for each white youth

TAKEN FROM: Human Rights Watch, *When I Die, They'll Send Me Home: Youth Sentenced to Life Without Parole in California*, January 2008.
http://www.hrw.org/reports/2008/us0108/us0108web.pdf.

quired to "address disproportionate minority contact efforts and system improvement efforts designed to reduce, without establishing or requiring numerical standards or quotas, the disproportionate number of juvenile members of minority groups, who come into contact with the juvenile justice system." In the current reauthorization for this law process, more expansive requirements are proposed in the U.S. Senate's reauthorization bill to develop steering committees, examine data, understand causes of disparities, and take steps to address them.

States use various methods to address disproportionate minority contact, including collecting data to determine the extent of the problem; establishing task forces and commissions to study policies to facilitate racially neutral decisions throughout the system; developing and expanding early intervention services for minority youth and their families; and creating alternatives to incarceration. . . .

Looking for Effective Solutions

As states continue to study and formulate disproportionate minority contact reduction policies, some common problems and effective strategies are emerging. Data collection is a common problem because race identification often is complex and personal. A standardized model for uniform data collection helps local data collectors accurately record and report information.

One important aspect of data collection is to recognize and record both race and ethnicity. Research suggests that, if ethnicity and race are not identified separately, Hispanic youth may be significantly undercounted. Guidelines from the National Center for Juvenile Justice and the Center for Children's Law and Policy suggest a series of questions—in addition to self-identification, observation and other sources such as court documents—to help obtain the most accurate and detailed documentation. Reliable data are important to effective analysis and development of appropriate solutions to reduce racial disparities.

Awareness is a critical aspect of reducing institutional biases. The Models for Change initiative strives to raise awareness about disproportionate minority contact among community representatives, leaders, parents and others. Some states have sponsored seminars and training sessions for prosecutors, judges, agency personnel and others involved in the juvenile justice process. According to OJJDP, 15 states have implemented cultural competency training and/or organizational cultural competency assessments. Many counties, parishes and cities also have implemented awareness programs.

In line with JJDPA's system-wide effort to addressing disproportionate minority contact, the Center for Children's Law and Policy and the Models for Change initiative suggest states analyze and address the problem at nine critical processing points. The Center for Children's Law and Policy encourages creation of an oversight body composed of stakeholders to identify where disparities exist, pinpoint unnecessary juvenile justice system involvement, and monitor implementation of reforms to address disproportionate minority representation.

Alternatives to Detention

Since attention to the use or secure detention is a critical point, focusing on it can help to reduce over-representation. A risk-assessment instrument can help avoid overuse of secure detention, the holding of youth, upon arrest, in a juvenile detention facility, such as a juvenile hall, according to the Center for Children's Law and Policy. Reducing unnecessary detention of youth who pose little risk helps reduce minority detention and over-representation. The Juvenile Detention Alternatives Initiative has used risk-assessment instruments with measurable success in their local site programs, particularly in Multnomah County, Oregon.

Appropriate use of alternatives to secure confinement of juveniles in correction facilities can be used to reduce disproportionate minority contact. These include community-based services and graduated parole violation sanctions. According to the Office of Juvenile Justice and Delinquency Prevention,

19 states currently use objective risk-assessment instruments, and 25 states fund alternatives to detention. Many counties, parishes and cities also have implemented such reforms.

Disproportionate minority contact remains a complex issue for states. The over-representation of young people of color in juvenile justice systems prompts questions about equality of treatment for youth by police, courts and other personnel in criminal and juvenile justice systems. How these juveniles are handled can significantly affect their development and future opportunities. States' attention to the issue, along with the research and resources of various private organizations, can strengthen efforts to reduce disproportionate minority contact and improve fairness for all youth in juvenile justice systems.

Periodical and Internet Sources Bibliography

The following articles have been selected to supplement the diverse views presented in this chapter.

Emily Bazelon	"They're Just Kids," *Slate*, May 17, 2010. www.slate.com.
Peter J. Benekos, Alida V. Merlo, and Charles M. Puzzanchera	"Youth, Race, and Serious Crime: Examining Trends and Critiquing Policy," *International Journal of Police Science & Management*, Summer 2011.
Jennifer Bishop-Jenkins	"Testimony to the United States Congress Re: HR 2289 'The Juvenile Justice and Accountability Act of 2009,'" National Organization of Victims of Juvenile Lifers, June 9, 2009. www.jlwopvictims.org.
Julia Dahl	"Throw-Away Children: Juvenile Justice in Collapse," The Crime Report, February 9, 2010. www.thecrimereport.org.
Jeffrey Fagan	"The Contradictions of Juvenile Crime and Punishment," *Daedalus*, Summer 2010.
Martha T. Moore	"Youth Prison System Under Pressure," *USA Today*, February 3, 2010.
Charles Ogletree	"Life Sentences for Juveniles Are Cruel and Unusual," *Bay State Banner*, November 12, 2009.
John Pitts	"Bringing the Boys Back Home: Youth Justice Reform from an Unexpected Quarter," *Safer Communities*, January 2010.
Maia Szalavitz	"Why Juvenile Detention Makes Teens Worse," *Time*, August 7, 2009.
Cal Thomas	"Life for Children," *Washington Times*, November 26, 2009.

OPPOSING
VIEWPOINTS®
SERIES

CHAPTER 4

What Policies Will Best Reduce Juvenile Crime?

Chapter Preface

Public attitudes toward juvenile crime and how best to address the problem have shifted over the years from viewing juveniles as worthy of rehabilitation and thus limiting juvenile contact with the justice system to seeing juvenile crime as a growing problem requiring strong measures to protect public safety. During the mid-1990s, some academics predicted a growing population of juvenile superpredators. Princeton public policy professor John Dilulio and Northeastern University criminology professor James Alan Fox characterized these juvenile predators as sociopaths with no conscience or fear of juvenile justice sanctions. To respond to this new juvenile superpredator, some policy makers promoted a shift toward a strict law-and-order approach, dubbed "get tough" policies. As a result, state legislatures adopted policies that increased the number of youth entering both the juvenile and adult criminal justice systems. One of the controversies in the juvenile justice debate is whether these "get tough" policies actually reduced juvenile crime.

Statistics show that juvenile violent crime began to drop after its peak in 1994. By 1996, Justice Department statistics indicated that juvenile arrests for violent crimes had dropped 12 percent. By 2004, the number of juvenile arrests had fallen 22 percent. Those who support the "get tough" approach argue that these statistics prove these policies clearly work; some assert that the reduction was comparable to the adult crime reduction following the implementation of three-strikes laws, in which extensive prison time—in many cases a life sentence—is required after a third felony conviction. According to Nina Salarno-Ashford, a former California prosecutor, "we're taking the worst off the streets, and it does lower re-offending. Some do recidivate, but the heavier sentences for top-end offenders help in the decline."[1]

Others recommend caution when interpreting these statistics. Those who support reform are quick to note that there was a rise in violent juvenile crime between 2004 and 2006. "I would venture that few of these get-tough reformers are willing to take credit for the increase," maintains Temple University psychology professor Laurence Steinberg, a specialist in adolescent development. Youth advocates argue that the causes of crime have less to do with law and policy changes and more to do with social changes. Indeed, many analysts agree that the rise in violent crime during the 1980s and 1990s was due largely to the crack cocaine epidemic that hit the nation's inner cities. For example, claims Jeffrey Butts, executive director of the Criminal Justice Research and Evaluation Center at the John Jay College of Criminal Justice, "If we go back to the 1970s and '80s, when New York was expanding the use of adult courts and prisons for juveniles, do you see a corresponding decline for youth crime in New York? No."[2] In fact, he explains, conclusive cause-and-effect evidence is impossible to reproduce.

Youth advocates argue that "get tough" juvenile justice policies have incarcerated juveniles in very dangerous, abusive places. Indeed, statistics on sexual victimization in youth facilities led to a shift toward juvenile justice reform. A Justice Department report indicated that six juvenile facilities had sexual abuse rates of 30 percent or higher. Moreover, youth advocates argue, incarceration increases the risk that juveniles will be convicted of subsequent crimes committed as adults. One study of the New York State juvenile justice system found that 85 percent of boys and 65 percent of girls who are incarcerated are later convicted of a felony as adults. According to Barry Krisberg, former president of the National Council on

1. Peter Katel, "Juvenile Justice," *CQ Researcher*, November 7, 2008.
2. *Ibid.*

Crime and Delinquency and senior fellow at the University of California, Berkeley, law school, "We have to recognize that incarceration of youth per se is toxic, so we need to reduce incarceration of young people to the very small dangerous few."[3]

Reformers and hard-liners continue to contest whether rehabilitative or strict juvenile justice policies best reduce juvenile crime. The authors in the following chapter debate these and other policies to reduce juvenile crime. As cash-strapped coffers at the state and local levels are having an impact on programs aimed to deter youth crime, examining which policies are best is of increasing importance.

3. Thomas J. Billitteri, "Youth Violence," *CQ Researcher*, March 5, 2010.

> "Changes made to most states' juvenile codes in the 1990s . . . strike a proper balance between protecting public safety, holding youth appropriately accountable . . . and rehabilitating youthful offenders."

Tough Juvenile Justice Policies Reduce Crime by Holding Juveniles Accountable

James C. Backstrom

Juvenile justice policies enacted in the 1990s to address the growing problem of youth violence are not in need of reform, argues James C. Backstrom in the following viewpoint. Indeed, he maintains, such programs protect public safety by holding juveniles accountable. Claims that states prosecute a majority of youth in adult courts are misleading; they do not take into account the fact that many states have a lower age of majority, Backstrom asserts. Prosecutors and judges nationwide carefully consider aggravating factors and mitigating circumstances when applying state juvenile justice policies, he concludes. Backstrom, county at-

torney in Hastings, Minnesota, is a board member of the National District Attorneys Association and co-chair of its juvenile justice committee.

As you read, consider the following questions:

1. Why does Backstrom claim that adult court prosecution in Jacksonville, Florida, may be the best thing that happened to troubled kids?

2. How many states does the author claim have a lower age of majority for purposes of criminal prosecution?

3. How does the author explain "blended sentencing" models?

I read with concern the recent commentary of Shay Bilchik [in the *Washington Times*][1] (December 16, 2007) urging reform of the so-called "get tough" policies of America's juvenile codes, including curtailing of the ability of states to transfer juveniles to adult court for prosecution. Mr. Bilchik's article was based upon some misleading facts and examples and reaches a misguided conclusion. America's juvenile justice system is not broken or in need of reform.

Striking a Proper Balance

The changes made to most states' juvenile codes in the 1990s were not overly harsh on juvenile offenders. Rather, these laws strike a proper balance between protecting public safety, holding youth appropriately accountable for their crimes and rehabilitating youthful offenders. Contrary to the implications in Mr. Bilchik's article, the vast majority of youthful offenders in America are prosecuted in juvenile court. Few jurisdictions in our country prosecute more than 1–2% of juvenile offenders as adults and in some jurisdictions this statistic is even lower.

1. Shay Bilchik is founder and director of the Center for Juvenile Justice Reform at Georgetown University's Public Policy Institute.

Also, few prosecutors in America would ever seek to charge as an adult a youth who merely sells marijuana, which was the misleading centerpiece example used by Mr. Bilchik.

Some exceptions exist, like the highly praised program in Jacksonville, Florida, where many youth charged with lower-level felonies are prosecuted in adult court. These youth, however, receive sentences to a segregated youth-only section of the county jail, where the primary focus of their incarceration is on education and rehabilitation. This "adult court prosecution" may well be the best thing that ever happens to these troubled kids. Since this program was implemented, juvenile crime in the Jacksonville area has dropped significantly.

Statistical Fallacies

One of the primary fallacies of statistics misused by Mr. Bilchik and others to suggest that too many juveniles are prosecuted as adults in America is that these statistics are based upon using age 18 as the age of criminal majority. This is not the reality in all states in America. In fact, 13 states have a lower age of majority for purposes of criminal prosecution, and yet in computing the statistics as to the number of "juveniles" prosecuted as adults, 16- or 17-year-old youth in these states who are adults under the law are treated as if they were juveniles transferred to the adult system. That is why the statistic claiming that 200,000 or more "juveniles" are prosecuted as adults each year in America for minor crimes is meaningless unless the age of majority issue is properly factored into such an analysis.

The simple fact of the matter is that juveniles who commit serious and violent crimes, particularly older youth, should in most instances face adult court sanctions. So, too, must this remedy be available for youth who have committed less serious felonies who have a long history of convictions for crime after crime for which no juvenile court disposition has been

Curbing an Explosion in Violent Crime

Each year about 200,000 defendants under 18 are sent directly or transferred to the adult system, known as criminal court, according to rough estimates.

Most end up there because of state laws that automatically define them as adults, due to their age or offense. Their ranks rose in the 1990s as juvenile crime soared and legislators responded; 48 states made it easier to transfer kids into criminal court, according to the juvenile justice center.

These changes gave prosecutors greater latitude (they could transfer kids without a judge's permission), lowered the age or expanded the list of crimes that would make it mandatory for a case to be tried there.

Some states also adopted blended sentences in which two sanctions can be imposed simultaneously; if the teen follows the terms of the juvenile sentence, the adult sentence is revoked.

The changes were ushered in to curb an explosion in violent crime—the teen murder arrest rate doubled from 1987 to 1993 as the crack trade and guns flourished—and to address mounting frustrations with the juvenile justice system.

Sharon Cohen,
"Prosecuting Kids as Adults: Some States Ponder Changes",
USA Today, *December 2, 2007.*

effective. I believe that if this question is fairly framed, as it seldom is in discussions of this important topic, most Americans would agree.

A Fair and Thoughtful Approach

The National District Attorneys Association (NDAA) supports a balanced approach to juvenile justice which properly takes into consideration all relevant factors in deciding what criminal charge should be filed against a juvenile offender and whether the case should be disposed of in juvenile or adult court or handled under a "blended sentencing" model in those states incorporating this middle-ground approach of addressing juvenile crime. "Blended sentencing" models, which have been endorsed by the NDAA, currently exist in 15 states in America and represent a combination of both juvenile and adult criminal sanctions for serious, violent or habitual juvenile offenders whose crimes have been determined by either a prosecutor or a judge to not warrant immediate prosecution in adult court.

Articles such as Mr. Bilchik's reflect an inappropriate attack upon America's juvenile codes and wrongly cast aspersions upon prosecutors and judges who thoughtfully and professionally enforce those codes with fairness and impartiality every day. Not only are mitigating factors such as a juvenile offender's age and maturity and amenability to treatment and probation properly considered in the decision-making process at every stage of the handling of a juvenile crime, including whether juvenile offenders should properly face adult court sanctions for their actions, so too must aggravating factors be considered, such as the severity of the crime, the threat to public safety, the impact upon the victims and the offender's criminal history. These factors are properly weighed in the decision-making process each and every day by prosecutors and judges throughout America, and as a result, America's system of juvenile justice is properly balanced and not in need of reform.

> *"Too often our response to troubled youth, in the form of local and state juvenile justice systems, does much more harm than good."*

Alternatives to the Punishment-Oriented Juvenile Justice Model Are Necessary

Liane Gay Rozzell

In the following viewpoint, Liane Gay Rozzell claims that costly punishment-oriented juvenile justice responses to troubled youth increase the likelihood that they will re-offend, often more violently. Youth imprisoned for nonviolent offenses are often abused by prisoners and guards, she maintains. Moreover, the only lessons these youth learn is how to be more criminal. Proven community-based and restorative justice models give youths a chance to take responsibility for their actions and learn to be productive adults, she concludes. Rozzell is executive director of Families & Allies of Virginia's Youth.

As you read, consider the following questions:

1. According to Rozzell, how much does it cost per child per year to imprison youth in facilities like the one where her son was incarcerated?

2. What statistics does the author cite to support her claim that huge racial and ethnic disparities characterize the US juvenile justice system?

3. What restorative justice practices does the author identify?

When young people commit offenses, adults must respond—but too often our response to troubled youth, in the form of local and state juvenile justice systems, does much more harm than good.

Harmful Programs

One big problem: About 200,000 youth are prosecuted as adults each year, most for nonviolent offenses. Some of them are kids like Jay, a 14-year-old who was held in an adult jail to await trial. Too young to be admitted to the jail's GED [General Educational Development] course, Jay spent 15 months locked up without any education or programs. After he was finally found not guilty, his grandmother struggled to get him into a school where he could make up for lost time and heal from the trauma of being jailed with adults.

Children who spend time in adult prisons and jails are at much higher risk for assault, abuse, and suicide. They don't get the services they need, and they are more likely to reoffend—sooner, more often, and more violently—than youth who stay in the juvenile system.

We are also wrong to spend so much money and effort incarcerating young people in juvenile prisons or "training schools"—again, often for nonviolent offenses. My son was one of them. He was not a danger to the public, but was sent to a youth prison, where he was beaten by gang members and subjected to abuse and harassment by guards. Facilities like that one, which costs state taxpayers more than $102,000 per child per year, are abysmal failures, with high recidivism rates. Imprisoning kids to "teach them a lesson" is an almost surefire way of teaching them how to be more criminal.

Our public school systems have also contributed to the problem by adopting punitive "zero tolerance" policies and relying on police officers to enforce discipline, helping to create a "school to prison pipeline" for an increasing number of students, especially poor youth and youth of color. Schools are no safer, but students are being arrested for acts that used to be resolved by a trip to the principal's office, after-school detention, or suspension.

We have also come to rely on the juvenile justice system to deal with youth whose primary issues are mental illness, substance abuse, and trauma. Up to 70 percent of youth in the system suffer from mental health disorders.

Finally, huge racial and ethnic disparities characterize the juvenile justice system: Although minorities make up one-third of U.S. youth, they are almost two-thirds of those who are locked up. Youth of color are treated more harshly than white youth in all parts of the system.

Giving Youth a Chance to Change

How should we respond to delinquent young people? By using the growing body of cost-effective, evidence-based programs that give youth a fair chance to change, to heal, to take responsibility for their actions, and to develop into positive, productive adults.

Proven, smarter, saner, and safer alternatives to the failed punishment-oriented model include community-based prevention and intervention programs built on a positive youth development model (which builds on a youth's strengths

175

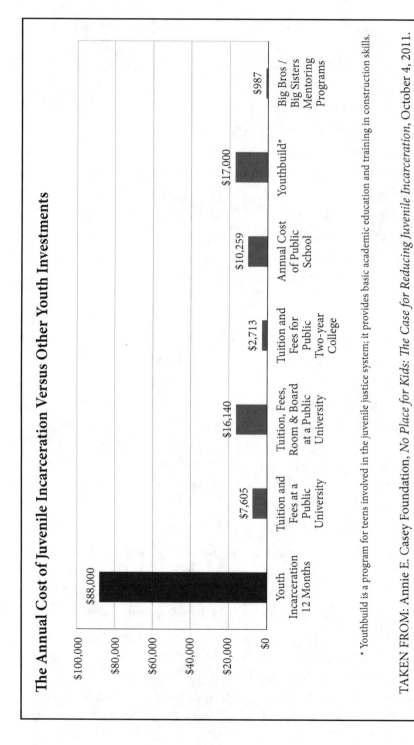

The Annual Cost of Juvenile Incarceration Versus Other Youth Investments

Youth Incarceration 12 Months	$88,000
Tuition and Fees at a Public University	$7,605
Tuition, Fees, Room & Board at a Public University	$16,140
Tuition and Fees for Public Two-year College	$2,713
Annual Cost of Public School	$10,259
Youthbuild*	$17,000
Big Bros / Big Sisters Mentoring Programs	$987

* Youthbuild is a program for teens involved in the juvenile justice system; it provides basic academic education and training in construction skills.

TAKEN FROM: Annie E. Casey Foundation, *No Place for Kids: The Case for Reducing Juvenile Incarceration*, October 4, 2011.

rather than focusing solely on deficiencies); wraparound social services; and family-focused therapeutic interventions.

The juvenile justice reform movement is making progress. Communities all over the country are safely reducing their reliance on locked facilities. Some have begun to reduce racial disparities in their juvenile justice systems, using tools such as screenings that cut bias in detention admission decisions. For nonviolent youth, day and evening reporting centers provide a place where they can be supervised and gain skills before their court hearings.

Some communities are turning to restorative justice practices—including peer juries, peacemaking circles, and family group conferencing—to create better outcomes for victims, offenders, and the community. Schools that adopt positive behavior support, which systematically reinforces and rewards good behavior, are creating peaceful learning environments—and boosting achievement.

A stronger Juvenile Justice and Delinquency Prevention Act, currently before Congress, would drastically reduce the number of youth who are locked in detention for truancy or being runaways, push states to keep children out of adult jails, and require states to do more to reduce ethnic disparities. Legislators are also considering the Youth PROMISE Act,[1] which would fund effective, community-chosen approaches to preventing and curbing delinquency.

We will only succeed when we stop demonizing and discarding troubled youth. These are our children. For our sake and theirs, we must take responsibility for how we respond to them.

---

1. Neither the Juvenile Justice and Delinquency Prevention Reauthorization Act of 2009 or the Youth Prison Reduction through Opportunities, Mentoring, Intervention, Support, and Education (PROMISE) Act became law.

> "Pursuit of a civil gang injunction . . . offers a potent tool to prosecutors, members of law enforcement and local communities."

Civil Injunctions Are an Effective Way to Fight Gang Crime

Whitney Tymas

Civil gang injunctions create penalties for offensive gang behaviors not defined as crimes, asserts Whitney Tymas in the following viewpoint. The civil gang injunction is based on the doctrine of public nuisance that prohibits behaviors that interfere with people's right to peacefully enjoy their property or freely walk the streets, she explains. The injunction prohibits gang members from associating, which has the effect of limiting their ability to engage in such public nuisance activities as graffiti, vandalism, and drug dealing. This viewpoint summarizes the work of Max Shiner, Los Angeles deputy city attorney. Tymas is senior attorney in the Community Prosecution and Project Safe Neighborhoods programs of the National District Attorneys Association.

Whitney Tymas, "The Civil Gang Injunction: An Innovative Approach to Targeting Gang Activity," *Swift & Certain*, vol. 5, 2010. Copyright © 2010 by National District Attorneys Association. All rights reserved. Reproduced by permission.

As you read, consider the following questions:

1. According to Tymas, how does the California Civil Code define a nuisance?

2. What test do courts use to determine whether harm to the community is substantial?

3. What does the author say prosecutors must provide when seeking a civil gang injunction?

With a nationwide escalation of criminal street gangs, prosecutors, members of law enforcement and allied professionals have sought to develop innovative methods of addressing the criminal activities of these groups and their crippling effects on local communities. One approach, pioneered by the Los Angeles City Attorney's Office, is the use of the civil gang injunction. . . .

A Hybrid Law

The civil injunction, while a new tool for most prosecutors, has its antecedents in the common law[1] doctrine of public nuisance. Today, in all states, either a common law or statutory cause of action[2] lies for public nuisance, which involves some injury to or interference with rights common to the public.

While grounded in civil law,[3] the gang injunction is part of an effective strategy that also employs criminal sanctions. Once a prosecutor is successful in convincing a court that

1. Common law is created from legal precedent that is established in rulings on the facts in legal cases. In addition, customs and practices held by the community are often considered common laws.
2. Statutory laws are created by governments and legislatures. A cause of action is the set of facts that lead to the belief that legal relief is available.
3. Civil law generally deals with disputes between private parties, while criminal law deals with crimes against the public conscience, often established by criminal laws. Crimes may be against the person—rape, robbery, murder—but they are public crimes because they offend the community's moral and ethical beliefs as established by laws.

conduct or a condition rises to the level of a public nuisance, he or she may seek an order granting injunctive relief. Failure to obey the court's order is usually treated as criminal contempt of court, in many instances conferring upon law enforcement the ability to arrest and search on the spot. In this regard, the gang injunction is a hybrid—a civil measure used as part of an overall strategy that offers prosecutors the leverage of the criminal process.

A Strategy Tested in California

California prosecutors have pursued this strategy, invoking public nuisance law with frequency. California Civil Code, section 3479, defines nuisance as:

> Anything which is injurious to health, including but not limited to, the illegal sale of controlled substances or is indecent or offensive to the senses or an obstruction to the free use of property, so as to interfere with the comfortable enjoyment of life or property, or unlawfully obstructs the free passage or use, in the customary manner, of any navigable lake, or river, bay, stream, canal, or basin, or any public park, square, street, or highway, is a nuisance.

Further, California Civil Code, section 3480, defines public nuisance as:

> [O]ne which affects an entire community or neighborhood, or any considerable number of persons, although the extent of the annoyance or damage inflicted upon individuals may be unequal.

A virtually identical provision of the California Penal Code defines public nuisance as a crime. . . .

States vary in their definitions of public nuisance. While the California code is typical of some states' laws in presenting a wide range of activities that may constitute a public nuisance, others have defined the offense with particularity, enacting statutes proscribing specific conduct or conditions that interfere with the rights of the general public. Still other states and localities have passed statutes or ordinances defining certain conduct as a nuisance *per se* [meaning that certain types of conduct, by the specific definition in the law, are a nuisance]. Whatever the scheme, in each state, there may exist either a common law or statutory cause of action for public nuisance that an injunction may remedy. . . .

For an activity to be actionable as a public nuisance, it must rise above the level of a "trifling annoyance" such that the interference with public rights is "substantial and unreasonable." In other words, there must be a real and appreciable invasion of a plaintiff's interests. Courts generally use an objective test to determine whether the harm is substantial, asking whether a reasonable person would consider the invasion at issue unreasonable. Significantly, if a plaintiff's apprehension of injury is such that it interferes with the comfortable enjoyment of life or property, a defendant's conduct need not cause actual harm to be actionable.

In the context of gang prevention and suppression, specifically, the prosecutor must be able to prove, through documentary and testimonial evidence, that the gang, by its members' ongoing criminal conduct within a defined geographic area, is causing actual or threatened harm. Examples of such conduct might include graffiti, vandalism, drive-by shootings or drug distribution.

The Provisions of a Gang Injunction

In general, a gang injunction will have multiple provisions, the most important of which is the "do not associate" requirement. This requirement restricts gang members' ability to gather in groups in public. As a result, it serves to deter their ability to act collectively—an aspect of gang behavior that amplifies its threatening and dangerous nature.

Other common gang injunction provisions include prohibitions on: intimidation; possession of firearms; possession of imitation firearms or dangerous weapons; illegal sale, proximity to and possession or use of controlled substances or related paraphernalia; possession of alcohol; trespassing; curfew violations; graffiti or possession of graffiti tools; forcible recruiting; preventing a member from leaving the gang; and failing to obey all laws.

Notably, certain provisions, such as the requirement that an enjoined gang member stay away from drugs, place a burden on that individual to remove himself from any place where he knows drugs are present. Significantly, this provision may eliminate the requirement that a prosecutor prove possession when narcotics are present among a group of gang members.

Looking at Ethical and Strategic Considerations

Constitutional challenges to gang injunctions have abounded in California and have included attacks based on the First Amendment's right to free association, vagueness, and overbreadth. While California's Supreme Court has found that gang injunctions pass constitutional muster, prosecutors from other states are encouraged to study California law in anticipation of challenges to their own gang injunction efforts. It is possible the constitutions of other states may confer a broader right to free association than the United States or California constitutions do.

Care should also be taken in selecting a target gang. . . . The conduct and activities of its members must indeed, constitute a public nuisance for pursuit of a civil gang injunction to be an appropriate strategy.

In addition, it is likely that any criminal street gang's harmful conduct will fall within some category of activity constituting a nuisance. Hence, a prosecutor should be prepared to work strategically with investigators to obtain and marshal extensive, varied evidence of a gang's activities to meet the definition of public nuisance applicable in that jurisdiction. Further, a gang must have identifiable members, and documentation of their activities must be available. Finally, a prosecutor should be mindful that, in seeking a civil gang injunction, it will be necessary to provide testimony from an officer with suitable experience, knowledge, training and familiarity with the gang in question to be qualified under the rules of evidence as a gang expert. The expert's declaration in support of the injunction may be the single most important document provided to the court and may determine the nature and scope of relief granted.

Ultimately, the success of a civil gang injunction requires careful planning and coordination between the prosecution and law enforcement, such that all necessary decisions are made well before a case is ever filed.

Pursuit of a civil gang injunction is a time- and labor-intensive endeavor. Nonetheless, this approach to targeting gang activity offers a potent tool to prosecutors, members of law enforcement and local communities.

> "Civil injunctions against gangs do not improve public safety and . . . such policies often unfairly target youth and communities of color."

Civil Injunctions Are the Wrong Way to Fight Gang Crime

Tracy Velázquez

Civil gang injunctions do not improve public safety, argues Tracy Velázquez in the following viewpoint. In fact, she claims, they may make matters worse. Injunctions often target minority youth and their communities; for that reason and others, injunctions tend to heighten tension between the community and police. Although Los Angeles has been using gang injunctions for years, the city remains a hotbed of gang activity, she maintains. In addition, labeling youth as gang members based on loose definitions creates barriers to education and employment. Programs that invest in positive alternatives for youth are a better way to spend public money, she concludes. Velázquez is executive director of the Justice Policy Institute, which opposes sweeping anti-gang policies.

As you read, consider the following questions:

1. How has New York reduced gang crime, according to Velázquez?

2. What did research published by the Justice Department find about gang members, according to the author?

3. What percentage of black men aged twenty-one to twenty-four in Los Angeles were entered into the city's gang database in 2003?

This Memorial Day [2009], the District [of Columbia] is starting the summer with a decline in crime. Homicides are down 22.6 percent from the same point a year ago, according to the D.C. police department, and violent crime in general is running about 3 percent below last year.

Despite this good news, some neighborhoods continue to experience higher rates of violence. Two bills—one by D.C. Council member Phil Mendelson, the other by Mayor Adrian M. Fenty—are attempting to address this violence by creating far-reaching "anti-gang" policies.[1] Unfortunately, because these policies don't follow the research on how to effectively prevent youth violence, they aren't likely to work and may in fact make our city less safe. Specifically, research has found that civil injunctions against gangs do not improve public safety and that such policies often unfairly target youth and communities of color.

A gang injunction is a judicial order that prevents people identified as gang members from congregating in public spaces within a certain area and that creates additional restrictions on otherwise legal activities. This is not a new concept: Los Angeles has used injunctions and other suppression tactics for years. Yet L.A. remains the gang capital of the world. In contrast, New York City chooses to address gang-related crime through increased street work and gang-intervention pro-

1. As of late 2011, the D.C. Council continued to reject anti-gang injunction policies.

grams. As a result, crime there has fallen to historic lows, with gang-related offenses just a blip on the New York crime scene.

The Consequences of Gang Injunctions

How can punitive anti-gang policies, such as injunctions, reduce public safety? First, increased law enforcement and the aggressive stop-and-search techniques often associated with injunctions can increase tension between the community and police. Community members may become reluctant to cooperate with law enforcement. Also, permanent injunctions may actually reinforce gang affiliation, making it more difficult for youths to move on to become productive, law-abiding adults. Research published by the Justice Department has found that "gang membership tends to be short-lived, even among high-risk youth . . . with very few youth remaining gang members throughout their adolescent years." But the consequences of a permanent gang injunction can last a lifetime.

Injunctions may also have the unintended consequence of making it harder for young people to participate in positive social institutions that expose them to role models and healthier patterns of behavior. And the reluctance of mainstream social institutions to embrace former gang members and other people with criminal records means youths who are now being labeled as gang members—often based on loose definitions that can include three kids engaging in nuisance behavior—may face long-standing barriers to education and employment. That makes leaving the gang life behind even more difficult.

Targeting Youth of Color

Besides failing to improve public safety, anti-gang policies such as injunctions often unfairly target youths of color. Police can misidentify youths as gang members based solely on race, ethnicity, style of dress or association with others labeled as gang members. This can have serious consequences, par-

What Are Gang Injunctions?

Gang injunctions are a rapidly proliferating police tool even though they have not been proven effective. The first gang injunction was filed in Los Angeles in 1987, and since then there have been over 60 gang injunctions filed in [California]. The constitutionality of gang injunctions is still being contested.

A gang injunction is a civil suit filed against a group of people considered a "public nuisance," prohibiting them from participating in certain activities, usually including:

- Appearing in public with anyone police have labeled a "gang member" (including those not named in the injunction). Exceptions are supposed to be made for church, school and work.

- Being outside during 10pm–5am curfew, exceptions same as above.

- Loitering.

- Possessing graffiti paraphernalia including felt tip markers.

- Possessing or being in the presence of anyone possessing firearms, drugs, or drug paraphernalia including rolling papers.

- Wearing colors that police associate with the street organization in question.

"Betraying the Model City:
How Gang Injunctions Fail Oakland,"
Critical Resistance Oakland, February 2011.

ticularly for communities of color. In Los Angeles, for example, nearly half of all black men ages 21 to 24 were entered into a gang database in 2003. Clearly, those engaging in serious criminal behavior need to be held accountable, but branding a swath of kids through an injunction will do lasting harm to D.C. families and neighborhoods.

The District should focus its resources on strengthening youth employment and summer programs rather than on punitive policies that wall off communities, harm minorities, and waste money and public safety resources. It's time to concentrate on implementing real solutions to the city's public safety challenges. Providing positive alternatives is an investment in youth and the most effective way of increasing safety for our communities and families.

> "Those kids who receive less than firm, fair, and consistent discipline end up being taught that there are no consequences for inappropriate—and sometimes illegal—behavior."

Strict but Reasonable Discipline Policies Are Necessary to Make Schools Safe

Ken Trump

In recent years, programs emphasizing security and discipline in schools have come under attack in the media and by politicians and scholars, asserts Ken Trump in the following viewpoint. Joining the chorus of voices that have blamed zero-tolerance policies for overly harsh punishments by some school administrators, these critics maintain that intervention and prevention programs are more effective than policies that emphasize discipline and employ metal detectors, surveillance, and the like. Trump acknowledges that intervention and prevention are important aspects of a school security program, but he asserts that firm, fair, and consistent discipline must be central components of any such program. In his experience, most school administrators are fair and firm in disciplinary policies, but those who are too lax or who fail to impose discipline consistently can cause as much harm as those who are overly strict. Trump maintains the importance of moving beyond the rhetoric of the zero-tolerance debate and implementing balanced, commonsense security solutions in schools. Trump, a school safety consultant, is author of Classroom Killers? Hallway Hostages? How Schools Can Prevent and Manage School Crises.

As you read, consider the following questions:

1. What is the real problem in cases labeled "zero tolerance" by critics, according to Trump?

2. In the author's view, in what way do academic and think tank reports usually err?

3. Upon what do anti-security and anti-police arguments rest, in the author's opinion?

"Zero tolerance" has been a political buzzword for so many years now that it has more meaning in the minds of academicians and politicians than it does in day-to-day practice by school administrators.

In well over 25 years of school safety experience with school officials in 50 states, we have consistently found the vast majority of school administrators to strive for firm, fair, and consistent discipline applied with good common sense. Unfortunately, there are anecdotal incidents from time to time which lack the latter part of the equation: the common sense.

It is these cases that get labeled as "zero tolerance" by critics who falsely try to create a perception that there is some type of mass conspiracy by educators to unfairly discipline children. Contrary to suggestions by the media, politicians, and ivory-tower theorists, the real problem is therefore the absence of common sense and questionable implementation of disciplinary policies, not the presence of intentionally harsh actions committed to fuel a master nationwide conspiracy plan called "zero tolerance."

Schools have also developed tunnel-vision focus in training school administrators on how to improve test scores, but often fail to provide adequate training on discipline and school safety issues. Proper training of school administrators on school board policies, disciplinary procedures, and overall school safety issues can reduce the risks of questionable actions by school administrators.

Lax, Not Harsh Discipline

If anything, our experience has shown that just the opposite exists: Many educators tend to bend over backwards to give students more breaks than they will ever receive out on the streets of our society and in the workplace where we are supposed to be preparing them to function. We can count many, many more instances where we have seen far too lax discipline in our schools than we can count cases where the discipline administered was overly harsh and abusively punitive as some critics want to suggest.

In the end, those kids who receive less than firm, fair, and consistent discipline end up being taught that there are no consequences for inappropriate—and sometimes illegal—behavior as long as it occurs within the grounds of those schools having administrators who are often more worried about keeping their disciplinary and criminal incident reports down for the sake of their own career advancement.

To keep it in perspective, the vast majority of school administrators strive for that target of firm, fair, and consistent discipline. The average school administrator is not an extremist on either end of the continuum.

Discrediting School Security Practices

Perhaps most alarming is how the zero-tolerance phrase has taken on a life of its own and how it has been exaggerated for the purpose of either supporting or opposing other school safety strategies. For example, academic and "think tank" reports use zero tolerance as a backdrop to promote prevention programs while discrediting school security practices.

These reports typically err, however, by inaccurately and narrowly defining school security to mean metal detectors, surveillance cameras, school security personnel, school resource officers (SROs) or other police in schools, locker searches, and/or school uniforms. Most school security specialists agree that professional school security programs are much more comprehensive and include security policies and procedures, crime prevention training, crisis preparedness planning, physical design evaluation, coordination with public safety officials, and numerous other components. While these other tools and strategies may be a necessary and appropriate part of many school safety plans, truly professional school security programs are much more encompassing than one or two single approaches.

It is also particularly interesting that the primary basis for many of these reports' anti-security and anti-police arguments rest upon the absence of formal academic studies of school security and school policing programs. Ironically, these reports typically fail to also point out that a number of academic evaluations have identified major weaknesses in many prevention and intervention programs, too, and in some cases have indicated that a number of those programs evaluated are simply ineffective. Yet the authors of these reports condemn school security programs (under the guise of zero tolerance) while continuing to promote prevention programs simply because there have indeed been formal evaluations of prevention programs—regardless of the mixed evaluation findings.

Reasonable Discipline Measures

Practical experience repeatedly demonstrates that school safety plans need to reflect a balance of strategies focused on prevention, intervention, school climate, firm and fair discipline, mental health support, proactive security measures, crisis preparedness planning, and community networking. Reasonable security and discipline measures must be a part of these plans so that educators can maintain a secure environment in the here-and-now in order for education and prevention programs to have their longer-term impact in the future. Furthermore, professionally utilized SRO and security personnel, security technology, and related measures can and do, in many cases, reduce risks and prevent school violence.

Zero tolerance has taken on a life of its own, but primarily by politicians, academicians, and in some cases the media. We owe it to our students, school staff, and parents to get beyond the political and academic rhetoric of the zero-tolerance debate. Improve training for school administrators on board discipline policies, implement student code of conducts fairly and consistently with common sense, and improve school safety in a balanced and rational manner. Deal with each individual case of questionable discipline, but move on to the real work of implementing meaningful, balanced school safety programs such as those enacted by the majority of educators across the nation.

> "Zero-tolerance discipline polices are an-
> tithetical to social work values and a
> democratic society and harm a signifi-
> cant number of young people."

Zero-Tolerance Policies in
Schools Hurt At-Risk Youth

David R. Dupper

*In the following viewpoint, University of Tennessee social work
professor David R. Dupper asserts that zero-tolerance discipline
policies have led to an epidemic of school suspensions, especially
among minority youth. According to the author, such policies
have led to an alarming number of student arrests for minor
discipline problems. Zero-tolerance discipline policies criminalize
behavior and create a fearful environment, Dupper claims. Indeed, he argues, teachers can easily abuse vaguely defined phrases
such as insubordination. Since disciplinary suspensions increase
the dropout rate and put students on the path to future incarceration, officials should examine each case based on the situation and reserve suspension and expulsion for only serious, disruptive behavior, Dupper reasons.*

David R. Dupper, "Does the Punishment Fit the Crime? The Impact of Zero Tolerance
Discipline on At-Risk Youth," *Children & Schools*, vol. 32, April 2010, pp. 67–69. Copyright © 2010 by National Association of Social Workers, Inc. All rights reserved. Reproduced by permission.

As you read, consider the following questions:

1. What congressional legislation led to zero-tolerance policies, according to Dupper?

2. What does characterizing certain student interactions with adults as "insubordination" fail to take into account, in the author's view?

3. In the author's opinion, what must be included in a state's definition of weapon for there to be no question whether a suspension is warranted?

In response to disastrous, yet relatively rare, instances of deadly school violence, Congress, in 1994, passed the Gun-Free School Act (GFSA). The GFSA mandated that each state pass legislation that requires a one-year expulsion for any student who brings a firearm to school for schools to be eligible to receive certain federal education funding. This legislation resulted in the implementation of zero-tolerance policies and practices in the vast majority of U.S. public schools over the past decade. By the 1996–97 school year, 94 percent of U.S. public schools had zero-tolerance policies for firearms, 91 percent for other weapons, 88 percent for drugs, and 87 percent for alcohol. What impact has this increasing use of zero-tolerance discipline policies had on our most vulnerable, at-risk groups of students?

A Disproportionate Impact

The pervasive impact of zero-tolerance discipline policies and practices in today's U.S. public schools cannot be overstated. This tough and swift "one-size-fits-all" punishment has resulted in a near epidemic of out-of-school suspensions. Zero-tolerance discipline policies disproportionately affect African American and Hispanic students, who are suspended at approximately three times the rate of white students. These discipline policies have also resulted in alarming numbers of students being referred to law enforcement and being arrested for minor skirmishes. A striking example recently occurred in Chicago, when 25 students, ages 11 to 15, were "rounded up, arrested, taken from school and put in jail" for engaging in a food fight. In the not-too-distant past, situations such as these would have been handled by school officials, often leading to a detention or parent conference. The American Civil Liberties Union of Michigan (2009) recently issued a report titled "Reclaiming Michigan's Throwaway Kids: Students Trapped in the School-to-Prison Pipeline," which documents and analyzes data that show how the frequent use of suspensions and expulsions disproportionately affects African American students and contributes to their dropping out of school and how these increasingly severe disciplinary policies criminalize student behavior and place students on a high-risk path to incarceration. For example, on any given day, nearly one in 10 young male high school dropouts and one in four African American dropouts is either in jail or in juvenile detention.

A Culture of Fear and Social Control

Zero-tolerance discipline policies are antithetical to social work values and a democratic society and harm a significant number of young people. There used to be a time when discipline in schools involved listening, exploring underlying issues, and deciding on a disciplinary response that was connected to the nature of the offense. Today, reason and judgment have been replaced with discipline practices that criminalize student behavior and create a school culture of fear and social control.

The cumulative impact of zero-tolerance discipline policies is often insidious. For example, most would agree that students should be excluded from school for dangerous behaviors that pose a risk to others. However, there is evidence that out-of-school suspensions are not limited to only the most serious and dangerous student offenses. During the

The Zero-Tolerance Paradox

After nearly two decades of zero-tolerance and authoritarian discipline, the paradox persists. Why do schools with the most security measures and most punitive discipline still tend to have more reported incidents of violence or crime? If the punitive, policing approach were effective, then incidents and student suspensions should be going down. The fact that juvenile crime rates outside the schoolhouse continue to fall makes the situation inside even more incongruous.

Annette Fuentes, "Report from Lockdown High: Fear vs. Facts on School Safety," City Limits, March 11, 2011.

2005–06 school year, two categories of offenses—"insubordination" and "use or possession of a weapon other than a firearm or explosive device"—accounted for 40 percent of school student removals.

Criminalizing Insubordination

The most serious concerns and questions are in relation to insubordination. The vast majority of school districts in the United States have one or more of these vaguely defined catchall categories of behaviors that are used to remove a student from school. The major problem with vague catchall categories is that they include both major and minor offenses yet deal with all offenses in the same harsh manner. Characterizing certain student interactions with adults as "insubordination" fails to take into account the tolerance level of the adult and the context of a given adult-student interaction. For example, a student may openly challenge statements made by his teachers and be praised by one teacher for his or her critical thinking but "written up" by another teacher for "insubordination." As long as school officials are provided with the option of reporting student behaviors under broadly defined catchall categories such as insubordination, there will always be a question about whether a given student's behavior was serious enough to warrant a suspension or whether a teacher or administrator is misusing his or her authority to arbitrarily punish certain students, especially those students who continually challenge his or her authority. This is an important issue that may account for large and growing numbers of suspensions, especially among poor and minority students. To remedy this problem, catchall categories such as insubordination should not be used in reporting disciplinary offenses. Rather, states and local school districts should gather and report data that clearly define what students did as well as specific information on any disciplinary action taken by the school and the duration of the disciplinary action. As a general rule, disciplinary consequences should be geared to the seriousness of the student's infraction, with exclusionary practices such as suspensions and expulsions being reserved for the most serious and disruptive student behaviors.

Poorly Defined Terms

Another example of the insidious impact of zero-tolerance policies has to do with the definition of terms. At first glance, it would appear that an offense that falls under "use or possession of a weapon other than a firearm or explosive device" should always result in an automatic removal from school. Students who bring a gun, knife, or club to school should be removed from school. However, there is evidence that the definition of "weapons" may not be as clear-cut as these examples suggest. For example, [J.A.] Sughrue (2003) found that *weapons* in one Virginia school district was broadly defined to include "any instrument that could injure, harm or endanger the physical well-being of another person"; this definition lists a wide number of objects that would be considered weapons but also includes the statement that weapons are "not limited to" these objects. How many and what types of additional objects could be considered weapons under this definition? Could a state define any sharp pointed or edged instrument a weapon? Apparently so. Strict adherence to zero-tolerance policies has resulted in students being excluded from school for bringing items such as eyebrow trimmers and a Cub Scouts camping tool to school. Without specification of which specific objects are and which specific objects are not included in a state's definition of weapon, there will always be a question about whether a suspension was warranted in a given situation.

The impact of these draconian policies on the school dropout problem has been downplayed or ignored for too long. It is time for school social workers to become more aware of the detrimental impact of zero-tolerance discipline policies and practices in schools, especially for African American students, and to use this knowledge to advocate for effective alternatives to zero-tolerance discipline.

> *"Just because of their profession, teach-*
> *ers should not be forced into unarmed*
> *helplessness."*

Arming Teachers Is Necessary to Reduce School Violence

Ted Nugent

Students are increasingly violently attacking their teachers, and teachers have a right to protect themselves, argues Ted Nugent in the following viewpoint. To protect teachers and society from serious assaults by juveniles, teachers need to arm themselves; teachers should not have to be forced to become victims because they are unarmed, Nugent insists. The growing list of school shootings has taught us that people can be dangerous at any age, and we need to prepare ourselves, Nugent concludes. Rock legend Ted Nugent is noted for his conservative political views and his vocal pro-hunting and Second Amendment activism.

As you read, consider the following questions:

1. What is one critique the author gives of the juvenile justice system?

2. In the event that a teacher is violently attacked, what should the teacher have a right to do, in the opinion of the author?

3. What does "Nuge justice" say about violent juvenile crime?

The total lack of respect among some of the young punks roaming the streets of America is absolutely appalling. They have no respect for their teachers, parents, law enforcement, neighbors, America, the rule of law, any authority or themselves. Some punks have no respect for your life or their own pathetic lives, and that makes them extremely dangerous.

Rarely does a week go by that I don't read an article or hear of a teacher being attacked by one of these vicious punks in our schools. As I write this from moose camp in the Yukon territory, this past week [in October 2009] a teacher was stabbed to death in Tyler, Texas.

Assaults on Teachers

A quick search of the Internet reveals some very disturbing statistics regarding serious assaults on teachers by violent punks. Because these future convicts are subject to the pathetic and counterproductive so-called "juvenile justice system," their punishment rarely fits their very serious crimes, including murder, rape, first-degree assault and more.

Three critical things need to happen to protect our teachers and society from these future adult offenders.

First, teachers should have the right to be armed. In the event they are violently attacked by a violent punk, teachers should have the right and obligation to fill the punks with hot lead. Just because of their profession, teachers should not be forced into unarmed helplessness. No teacher should be forced to become a victim because of left-wing blowhards who have made discipline and order extinct in our public schools over the past 30 years. Liberal policies create victims.

Juveniles and Guns

- 17.5% reported carrying a weapon (gun, knife or club) on one or more days in the 30 days preceding the survey [referring to a 2009 Centers for Disease Control and Prevention survey of youths in grades nine through twelve].

- 5.9% carried a gun on one or more days in the 30 days preceding the survey.

- Males were more likely than females to carry a weapon (27.1% versus 7.1%) on one or more days in the 30 days preceding the survey.

- Males were also more likely than females to carry a gun on one or more days in the 30 days preceding the survey (9.8% versus 1.7%).

"Youth Violence: Facts at a Glance,"
Centers for Disease Control and Prevention, 2010.

Secondly, we should do away with the mandatory age of sixteen before a punk can quit school. If a parent is too dumb, stoned or both to care about ensuring their offspring get an education, then our public schools should not have to tolerate the teenage menaces in school. I wouldn't let them drop out of school. I would drop-kick them out of school.

The Juvenile Justice System

Most of these punks will either end up dead or be sent to prison anyway. The others will end up drunks, crackheads and baby makers. This is the truth and everyone knows it.

The juvenile justice system is abysmal. A New York City judge once said that the purpose of the juvenile justice system was to give liberal-thinking people a job. Beautiful. This so-called "justice" system is a coddling, excuse-making system that turns violent juvenile punks into violent adult punks. If this is a justice system, I'm a yodeler in a goat band.

Thirdly, Nuge justice [referring to the author's own theory on juvenile justice] says that if a young punk commits a violent crime, we give them serious time. Get them permanently off our streets and put them in cages where they belong. They can spend decades stamping out license plates and turning big rocks into small rocks for all I care.

Everyone knows this is the right approach to solving the problem. There isn't a violent offender in prison that did not have an arrest record a mile long when he was a juvenile. The "system" and everyone else knows that young, violent punks are going to turn into hard-core, violent, adult offenders. The only people who refuse to believe this are busy renting Michael Moore movies and smoking dope, crack and sniffing lead paint chips.

The sad part of this pathetic equation is that hardworking families are going to be ripped apart when one of their loved ones becomes another victim of one of these violent punks. Our criminal justice system and its engineered revolving door of recidivism have been created to guarantee victims. This is tragically unnecessary, but as you are reading these words, another law-abiding citizen has become a victim, or a paroled punk has been put on probation again. Another family will be emotionally crushed because our so-called justice system cares more about thugs and punks than law-abiding citizens.

Spare Innocent Lives

My solutions will work. Innocent lives will be spared and our classrooms and communities will be a safer place to live, learn, work and play. Who could not possibly want this besides out-of-touch liberals who will propose more tax dollars be thrown at the problem, more bureaucratic meddling, more teacher pay, more teacher unions, more coddling, more excuse making, more victims?

I want carjackers, rapists and murderers cut in half at the scene of the crime regardless of their age. Dialing 911 should be used to call in a cleanup crew to hose the remnants of the perpetrators down the sewer. Do you want to solve the problem or continue to jack around while more innocent lives are ruined?

Liberalism is a public cancer, and the sooner it is halted and their upside-down policies are made extinct, the sooner society can go about the business of building a better, more vibrant, and safer America that provides unlimited opportunity for those who want to celebrate it. Those who want to violently deny someone their opportunity to life, liberty and the pursuit of happiness should be made extinct.

"*As a society, do we really want our teachers to be prepared to shoot children, perhaps killing them?*"

Arming Teachers Will Not Reduce School Violence

Allen Rostron and Brian Siebel

Arming teachers is a bad idea, claim Allen Rostron and Brian Siebel in the following viewpoint. Indeed, the authors assert, there is no evidence that armed teachers save lives. Moreover, the gun lobby's oft-cited example of the shooting at the Appalachian School of Law in Virginia ended when the shooter ran out of bullets and an unarmed student tackled him, not when those with guns confronted him. Also, the authors suggest, if teachers were armed, they would likely be the shooter's first victim. It is unfair to ask teachers who are not trained police officers to make the difficult decision of when shooting a student is actually necessary, the authors conclude. Allen Rostron is a professor at the University of Missouri at Kansas City School of Law. Brian Siebel was a senior attorney with the Brady Center to Prevent Gun Violence at the time this viewpoint was written; he is currently the director of justice programs at the Alliance for Justice.

Allen Rostron and Brian Siebel, "No Gun Left Behind: The Gun Lobby's Campaign to Push Guns into Colleges and Schools," Brady Center to Prevent Gun Violence, May 2007, pp. 9–11. www.bradycampaign.org. Copyright © 2007 by Brady Center to Prevent Gun Violence. All rights reserved. Reproduced by permission.

As you read, consider the following questions:

1. According to the authors, what percentage of the time, on average, do police officers hit their intended target?

2. In the authors' view, what has been the effect of the expiration of the Federal Assault Weapons Ban?

3. How is arming pilots different from arming teachers, in the authors' view?

The gun lobby is . . . pushing to arm elementary and secondary school teachers. Their push to arm college students would also allow college faculty and staff to arm themselves.

A Bad Idea

There are a number of reasons why arming teachers is a bad idea. First, it is entirely speculation on the gun lobby's part that arming teachers (or students) will ever save lives. In the one example often cited by the NRA [National Rifle Association] and gun lobby groups—a January 2002 shooting at the Appalachian School of Law in Grundy, Virginia—it turns out that the assailant stopped shooting when his gun ran out of bullets, not because some individuals had retrieved their guns and confronted him. Indeed, Ted Besen, an unarmed student whom police believed to be the real hero of the incident, recently criticized former House Speaker Newt Gingrich for claiming students with guns had saved the day. Besen said: "Their guns had no effect on [the shooter.] I already had [the shooter] on the ground before they got their guns out."

Moreover, given the frequency with which innocent civilians are killed or injured in urban cross fire and soldiers are killed by friendly fire, it is equally plausible that creating a cross fire might cost additional lives. Indeed, even trained police officers, on average, hit their intended target less than 20% of the time. After the shooting at Virginia Tech [on April

By Bill Schorr, politicalcartoons.com.

16, 2007], the executive director of the Virginia Association of Chiefs of Police said: "I have my own concerns that, had there been a number of people who had been in that classroom with guns, [there could have been] additional persons killed just as a result of poor judgment calls." According to security professionals, there are numerous survival options for students, faculty, and staff when confronted with an armed attacker that do not involve carrying a gun and firing back at him.

Undesirable Outcomes

Second, if the person attacking a school knows that teachers may be armed, that would simply make the teacher the likely first victim. Teachers can hardly be expected to outdraw surprise assailants like in some Wild West gunfight fantasy. Assailants might also respond to armed teachers by increasing their own firepower or wearing flak jackets [such as a bulletproof vest]. A decade ago, two bank robbers in Los Angeles donned body armor and, using automatic weapons, held off practically the entire Los Angeles Police Department. Unfortunately, the expiration of the Federal Assault Weapons Ban and its attendant ban on ammunition magazines of more than 10 rounds has made it far easier for school assailants to increase the firepower they can bring to bear. Most of the magazines Seung Hui Cho [the shooter at Virginia Tech] used in his assault had at least 15 rounds, and at least one may have had 33 rounds, which Glock advertises for sale on its website.

Third, many of the shooters that have assaulted schools are students themselves. As a society, do we really want our teachers to be prepared to shoot children, perhaps killing them? Certainly everyone would want to stop the carnage inflicted by Seung Hui Cho at Virginia Tech, or by teenagers Eric Harris and Dylan Klebold at Columbine High School [on April 20, 1999], but what about the student that merely flashes a gun threateningly? In one recent school year, 2,143 elementary or secondary school students were expelled for bringing or possessing a firearm at school. In how many of those instances would an armed teacher have been tempted to shoot the student because of a perception of danger? Recently enacted laws lowering the threshold for CCW [carrying a concealed weapon] licensees to shoot others with their firearms have led to a host of unwarranted shooting incidents. Even trained police officers have shot people they momentarily thought were dangerous who turned out not to be. And what about fist or knife fights that occur at schools? Should teachers be drawing their guns and trying to intercede?

Fourth, arming teachers is not like arming pilots. Pilots' firearms are stored in a secured cockpit where access is very tightly controlled. Teachers would be forced to carry weapons into classrooms filled with children and teens, thus opening many more opportunities for the guns to fall into the wrong hands. If you counter this risk by requiring gun safes in each classroom, aside from the exorbitant cost, it makes it even less likely the gun could be used to stop a school shooting, given the time it would take to retrieve the weapon. Kim Campbell, president of the Utah Education Association, put it this way:

> I would be opposed to guns in school, period. No matter where I would put a gun in a classroom, a class full of little people would find it. And if it were locked up for safety, there would be no chance to get it.

Turning Schools into Fortresses

Arming teachers will tend to turn schools into fortresses and teachers into prison guards. Yet, presumably, teachers did not sign up for that duty. Teachers are not members of the armed forces or trained police officers. They are teachers. We need to find better ways to make classrooms safer than by introducing guns into them.

In the aftermath of the Columbine High School massacre in 1999, even NRA executive vice president Wayne LaPierre shot down the idea of introducing guns into schools before the amassed NRA membership:

> First, we believe in absolutely gun-free, zero-tolerance, totally safe schools. That means no guns in America's schools, period . . . with the rare exception of law enforcement officers or trained security personnel.

> We believe America's schools should be as safe as America's airports. You can't talk about, much less take, bombs and guns onto airplanes. Such behavior in our schools should be prosecuted just as certainly as such behavior in our airports is prosecuted.

This is one of the very few times we have agreed with Mr. LaPierre. Since he made this statement, however, the NRA has shown ambivalence about this issue.

Periodical and Internet Sources Bibliography

The following articles have been selected to supplement the diverse views presented in this chapter.

Eve M. Brank, Edie Greene, and Katherine Hochevar	"Holding Parents Responsible: Is Vicarious Responsibility the Public's Answer to Juvenile Crime?," *Psychology, Public Policy, and Law,* November 2011.
John Dilulio Jr.	"More Religion, Less Juvenile Crime," *Sojourners,* February 2010.
Frank DiMaria	"School Violence: When the School House Is a Jail House," *Hispanic Outlook in Higher Education,* July 11, 2011.
Jeffrey Fagan and Franklin E. Zimring	"Myths of Get-Tough Law," *Tampa Bay Times* (Florida), November 2, 2009.
Kareem Fahim	"Seeking to Intervene with Young Adults Before Crime Becomes a Way of Life," *New York Times,* March 3, 2009.
Sara Lipka	"With 'Restorative Justice,' Colleges Strive to Educate Student Offenders," *Chronicle of Higher Education,* April 17, 2009.
Christopher Paslay	"Less than 'Zero Tolerance,'" Philly.com, January 28, 2011. www.philly.com.
Camilla Pemberton	"Resettlement for Youth Offenders Must Be Planned Early," Community Care, March 22, 2010. www.communitycare.co.uk.
Wilson Riles	"Gang Injunctions: Ineffective, Expensive and Discriminatory," OaklandSeen, May 27, 2010. www.oaklandseen.com.
David B. Wood	"Why One City Is Spending More on Antigang Efforts Despite Budget Cuts," *Christian Science Monitor,* June 10, 2011.

For Further Discussion

Chapter 1

1. Wendy Murphy argues that juvenile crimes are becoming increasingly more brutal. Randall G. Shelden claims that the media exaggerate the severity of juvenile crimes by focusing on rare but brutal crimes and citing as fact the opinions of officials. What rhetorical strategy does each author use to support his or her view? Which strategy do you think is more persuasive? Explain.

2. Colleen O'Connor maintains that the number of violent teen girls in the criminal justice system is growing. Margaret A. Zahn and her colleagues dispute this claim, arguing that the behavior of teen girls has not changed; instead, a change in law enforcement policies explains why more girls are arrested for violent behavior. How does the evidence that the authors cite to support their views differ? Which evidence do you find more persuasive? Explain.

3. James C. Howell and his colleagues assert that youth gangs are a serious problem that should be monitored like a disease. Judith Greene and Kevin Pranis claim that the interpretation of youth gang data is often flawed, explaining that many homicides identified as gang related in fact serve personal, not gang, interests. Since Greene and Pranis argue that misunderstanding the prevalence of the problem could lead to poor policies, how might they challenge the gang-problem-as-disease analogy to support their view? How might Howell and his coauthors answer this challenge?

4. What rhetorical commonalities on both sides of the debate can you find in this chapter? Explain, citing from the viewpoints.

Chapter 2

1. The chapter authors debate the merit of several causes of juvenile crime and violence. Which cause do you think contributes most to the problem? Explain.

2. Carmela Lomonaco, Tia Kim, and Lori Ottaviano claim that new evidence shows a connection between teen violence and watching violent media. The editors of the *Lancet* argue, on the other hand, that many factors contribute to youth violence. How do the authors' views on what causes juvenile crime and violence inform the strategy that each claims will best address the problem?

3. Dwain C. Fehon maintains that juveniles who witness or experience violence in the home or in the community are more likely to be violent themselves. Curt Alfrey finds a correlation between single-parent homes and juvenile violence. Since Alfrey's views inform his recommended prevention strategies, how might Alfrey answer possible claims that a nonviolent, single-parent home might be preferable to a violent intact family home?

4. Izzy Kalman argues that bullying is a significant factor in school violence. Kay S. Hymowitz disputes this claim, arguing that wasteful anti-bullying programs are based on widely accepted myths about the Columbine school shooting. What rhetorical strategies do the authors use to support their claims? Is one strategy more effective? Explain.

Chapter 3

1. James C. Backstrom argues that some juveniles should be prosecuted as adults for serious offenses because they know the difference between right and wrong. The Campaign for Youth Justice claims, however, that putting youth in adult jails not only does not reduce crime, but these youth also do not receive the education adolescents need. How does each author view the role of the criminal jus-

tice system? How does this influence each author's rhetoric? Which viewpoint do you find more persuasive?

2. Both Dick Mendel and the National Juvenile Justice Network oppose policies that favor incarcerating juveniles. The evidence and reasoning each uses to support this view, however, differ. Is one rhetorical strategy more persuasive in your view? Explain why or why not.

3. Charles D. Stimson and Andrew M. Grossman maintain that a majority of states have laws that allow juveniles to be sentenced to life without the possibility of parole. In their view, this demonstrates that most Americans believe that it is an appropriate punishment for violent juvenile criminals. Linda L. White argues that such policies ignore the differences between youth and adults and do not allow for rehabilitation. How do the authors' affiliations differ? Does each author's affiliation influence the viewpoint's persuasiveness? Explain why or why not.

4. What rhetorical strategy do Jeff Armour and Sarah Hammond use to support their claim that the juvenile justice system should address racial inequalities? Do you find this strategy persuasive?

Chapter 4

1. James C. Backstrom argues that tough juvenile justice policies are necessary to hold juveniles accountable for serious crimes and protect public safety. Liane Gay Rozzell counters that punishment-oriented policies actually increase violent re-offending. What evidence do the authors provide to support their claims? Which evidence do you find more persuasive?

2. Whitney Tymas asserts that civil law gang injunctions limit the gang's ability to engage in criminal activity. Tracy Velázquez maintains that civil law gang injunctions target minorities and create tension in minority communities. Note the affiliation of each viewpoint's author. How does

each author's affiliation inform her point of view? Does this make their views more or less persuasive? Explain why or why not.

3. Ken Trump claims that reasonable school discipline policies are necessary to make schools safe. David R. Dupper argues that zero-tolerance policies often lead to absurd penalties that criminalize behavior that is not disruptive. How does the rhetoric of each author differ? Which rhetorical strategy do you find more persuasive. Explain.

4. Ted Nugent claims that arming qualified, licensed teachers could reduce the carnage wrought by school shooters. Allen Rostron and Brian Siebel maintain that arming teachers has no proven impact on school shootings and could put students and teachers at greater risk. How does each author define the role of schoolteachers? How does this influence the authors' rhetoric? Which viewpoint do you find more persuasive? Explain.

5. What rhetorical commonalities on both sides of the debate can you find in this chapter? Explain, citing from the viewpoints.

Organizations to Contact

The editors have compiled the following list of organizations concerned with the issues debated in this book. The descriptions are derived from materials provided by the organizations. All have publications or information available for interested readers. The list was compiled on the date of publication of the present volume; the information provided here may change. Be aware that many organizations take several weeks or longer to respond to inquiries, so allow as much time as possible.

American Civil Liberties Union (ACLU)
125 Broad Street, 18th Floor, New York, NY   10004
(212) 549-2500
e-mail: infoaclu@aclu.org
website: www.aclu.org

The American Civil Liberties Union (ACLU) is a national organization that works to defend Americans' civil rights as guaranteed in the US Constitution. The ACLU works in courts, legislatures, and communities to defend First Amendment rights, the right to equal protection, the right to due process, and the right to privacy. The ACLU publishes the semiannual newsletter *Civil Liberties Alert,* as well as fact sheets, briefing papers, and reports, including "The Right to Education in the Juvenile and Criminal Justice Systems in the United States" and "The School to Prison Pipeline," which are available on its website.

Campaign for Youth Justice (CFYJ)
1012 Fourteenth Street NW, Suite 610
Washington, DC   20005
(202) 558-3580 • fax: (202) 386-9807
e-mail: info@cfyj.org
website: www.campaignforyouthjustice.org

The Campaign for Youth Justice (CFYJ) is dedicated to ending the practice of trying, sentencing, and incarcerating youth under eighteen in the adult criminal justice system. CFYJ advocates for juvenile justice reform by providing support to federal, state, and local campaigns; coordinating outreach to parents, youth, and families; fostering national coalition building; encouraging media relations; conducting research; and publishing reports and advocacy materials. On its website, CFYJ publishes reports and advocacy materials, including "Using *Graham v. Florida* to Challenge Juvenile Transfer Laws"; "The Consequences Aren't Minor: The Impact of Trying Youth as Adults and Strategies for Reform"; and "To Punish a Few: Too Many Youth Caught in the Net of Adult Prosecution."

Center for Children's Law and Policy (CCLP)

1701 K Street NW, Suite 1100, Washington, DC   20006
(202) 637-0377 • fax: (202) 379-1600
e-mail: infor@cclp.org
website: www.cclp.org

The Center for Children's Law and Policy (CCLP) is a law and policy organization whose goal is reform of juvenile justice and other systems that affect troubled and at-risk children, including the protection of their rights. The center conducts research; educates the public; and provides training, technical assistance, and administrative, legislative, and legal advocacy. CCLP also publishes resources on juvenile justice, many of which are available on its website, including "No More Children Left Behind Bars: A Briefing on Youth Gang Violence and Juvenile Crime," "Juvenile Transfer Laws: An Effective Deterrent to Delinquency?," and "Less Guilty by Reason of Adolescence."

Center for Juvenile Justice Reform (CJJR)

Georgetown Public Policy Institute, Georgetown University
3300 Whitehaven Street NW, Suite 5000, Box 571444
Washington, DC   20057
(202) 687-7657 • fax: (202) 687-7665
website: http://cjjr.georgetown.edu

The Center for Juvenile Justice Reform (CJJR) at Georgetown University's Public Policy Institute is designed to support public agency leaders in the juvenile justice and related systems of care. CJJR seeks to complement the work being done across the country in juvenile justice reform by providing a multi-systems perspective and set of resources in support of this work. The resources available at the center's website include "Supporting Youth in Transition to Adulthood: Lessons Learned from Child Welfare and Juvenile Justice" and "Safety, Fairness, Stability: Repositioning Juvenile Justice and Child Welfare to Engage Families and Communities."

Charles Hamilton Houston Institute for Race & Justice (CHHIRJ)

125 Mount Auburn Street, 3rd Floor
Cambridge, MA 02138-5765
(617) 495-8285 • fax: (617) 496-1406
e-mail: houstoninst@law.harvard.edu
website: www.charleshamiltonhouston.org

The Charles Hamilton Houston Institute for Race & Justice (CHHIRJ) honors and continues the work of one of the great civil rights lawyers of the twentieth century, Charles Hamilton Houston, who dedicated his life to using the law as a tool to reverse the unjust consequences of racial discrimination. One project of CHHIRJ, Redirecting the School to Prison Pipeline, focuses on understanding the journey for far too many children of color that begins in segregated, impoverished schools and ends in juvenile halls and adult prisons. Institute publications found on its website include the book excerpt "Beyond Zero Tolerance: Creating More Inclusive Schools by Improving Neighborhood Conditions, Attacking Racial Bias, and Reducing Inequality" and the brief "A Seamless Web of Support: Effective Strategies for Redirecting the School-to-Prison Pipeline."

Fight Crime: Invest in Kids

1212 New York Avenue NW, Suite 300
Washington, DC   20005
(202) 776-0027 • fax: (202) 776-0110
e-mail: info@fightcrime.org
website: www.fightcrime.org

Fight Crime: Invest in Kids is a national anticrime organization of more than three thousand police chiefs, sheriffs, prosecutors, other law enforcement leaders, and violence survivors. The organization focuses on early intervention crime prevention strategies and urges investment in programs proven effective by research. Fight Crime: Invest in Kids publishes numerous state and national reports on juvenile crime prevention, including "Proven Investment in Kids Will Prevent Crime and Violence" and "School or the Streets: Crime and America's Dropout Crisis."

Justice Policy Institute

1012 Fourteenth Street NW, Suite 400
Washington, DC   20005
(202) 558-7974 • fax: (202) 558-7978
e-mail: info@justicepolicy.org
website: www.justicepolicy.org

The goal of the Justice Policy Institute is to reduce the use of incarceration in the justice system and promote policies that improve the equitable treatment and well-being of all people and communities through just and effective solutions to social problems. In addition to broader criminal justice issues, the institute conducts research on issues concerning juvenile justice. Some of the publications on its Juvenile Justice link include the research reports "The Dangers of Detention: The Impact of Incarcerating Youth in Detention and Other Secure Facilities," "Gang Wars: The Failure of Enforcement Tactics and the Need for Effective Public Safety Strategies," and "Education Under Arrest: The Case Against Police in Schools."

National Council on Crime and Delinquency (NCCD)

1970 Broadway, Suite 500, Oakland, CA   94612
(800) 306-6233 • fax: (510) 894-6415
e-mail: info@sf.nccd-crc.org
website: www.nccd-crc.org

The National Council on Crime and Delinquency (NCCD) is a nonprofit criminal justice research organization that promotes effective, humane, fair, and economically sound solutions to family, community, and justice problems. NCCD conducts research; promotes reform initiatives; and works with individuals, public and private organizations, and the media to prevent crime and delinquency. NCCD publishes *Perspectives*, a seasonal newsletter, in addition to fact sheets and reports, many of which are available on its website, including "And Justice for Some: Differential Treatment of Youth of Color in the Justice System," "Youth in Gangs: Who Is at Risk?," and "Youth Violence Myths and Realities: A Tale of Three Cities."

Office of Juvenile Justice and Delinquency Prevention (OJJDP)

810 Seventh Street NW, Washington, DC   20531
(202) 307-5911
website: www.ojjdp.gov

The Office of Juvenile Justice and Delinquency Prevention (OJJDP), a component of the Office of Justice Programs of the US Department of Justice, collaborates with professionals from diverse disciplines to improve juvenile justice policies and practices. OJJDP accomplishes its mission by supporting states, local communities, and tribal jurisdictions in their efforts to develop and implement effective programs for juveniles. Through its Juvenile Justice Clearinghouse, OJJDP provides access to fact sheets, summaries, reports, and articles from its journal *Juvenile Justice*.

The Sentencing Project

1705 DeSales Street NW, 8th Floor, Washington, DC   20036
(202) 628-0871 • fax: (202) 628-1091
e-mail: staff@sentincingproject.org
website: www.sentencingproject.org

Dedicated to changing the way Americans think about crime and punishment, the Sentencing Project provides defense lawyers with training to reduce reliance on incarceration. The project leads the effort to bring national attention to disturbing trends and inequities in the criminal justice system and advocates for policy reform. On its Juvenile Justice website link, the project publishes articles, fact sheets, and reports, as well as links to other juvenile justice publications.

STRYVE (Striving to Reduce Youth Violence Everywhere)

Centers for Disease Control and Prevention
1600 Clifton Road, Atlanta, GA   30333
(800) 232-4636
e-mail: cdcinfo@cdc.gov
website: www.safeyouth.org

Formerly known as the National Youth Violence Prevention Resource Center, STRYVE is a national initiative led by the Centers for Disease Control and Prevention. The initiative takes a public health approach to preventing youth violence before it starts. To support community efforts to be successful in preventing youth violence, STRYVE provides access to training and information. On its website are fact sheets that define youth violence, provide data on the prevalence and consequences of youth violence, and report successful prevention strategies.

Bibliography of Books

Maryam
Ahranjani,
Andrew G.
Ferguson, and
Jamin B. Raskin

Youth Justice in America. Washington,
DC: CQ Press, 2005.

Meda
Chesney-Lind and
Katherine Irwin

*Beyond Bad Girls: Gender, Violence
and Hype.* New York: Routledge,
2007.

Michael A.
Corriero

*Judging Children as Children: A
Proposal for a Juvenile Justice System.*
Philadelphia, PA: Temple University
Press, 2006.

Finn-Aage
Esbensen et al.

*Youth Violence: Sex and Race
Differences in Offending,
Victimization, and Gang Membership.*
Philadelphia, PA: Temple University
Press, 2010.

Dorothy L.
Espelage and
Susan M. Swearer,
eds.

Bullying in North American Schools.
2nd ed. New York: Routledge, 2011.

Tom Grimes,
James A.
Anderson, and
Lori Bergen

*Media Violence and Aggression:
Science and Ideology.* Thousand Oaks,
CA: Sage Publications, 2008.

Bernard E.
Harcourt

*Language of the Gun: Youth, Crime,
and Public Policy.* Chicago: University
of Chicago Press, 2006.

Clayton A. Hartjen	*Youth, Crime, and Justice: A Global Inquiry*. New Brunswick, NJ: Rutgers University Press, 2008.
Steven J. Kirsh	*Children, Adolescents, and Media Violence: A Critical Look at the Research*. Thousand Oaks, CA: Sage Publications, 2006.
Susan Kuklin	*No Choirboy: Murder, Violence, and Teenagers on Death Row*. New York: Henry Holt, 2008.
Richard Lawrence	*School Crime and Juvenile Justice*. 2nd ed. New York: Oxford University Press, 2007.
Dennis Lines	*The Bullies: Understanding Bullies and Bullying*. Philadelphia, PA: Jessica Kingsley Publishers, 2008.
Marilyn D. McShane and Frank P. Williams III, eds.	*Youth Violence and Delinquency: Monsters and Myths*. Westport, CT: Praeger, 2007.
David L. Myers	*Boys Among Men: Trying and Sentencing Juveniles as Adults*. Westport, CT: Praeger, 2005.
Geoff Nichols	*Sport and Crime Reduction: The Role of Sports in Tackling Youth Crime*. New York: Routledge, 2007.
Anne M. Nurse	*Locked Up, Locked Out: Young Men in the Juvenile Justice System*. Nashville, TN: Vanderbilt University Press, 2010.

John A. Rich — *Wrong Place, Wrong Time: Trauma and Violence in the Lives of Young Black Men*. Baltimore, MD: Johns Hopkins University Press, 2009.

Laurie Schaffner — *Girls in Trouble with the Law*. New Brunswick, NJ: Rutgers University Press, 2006.

Elizabeth S. Scott and Laurence Steinberg — *Rethinking Juvenile Justice*. Cambridge, MA: Harvard University Press, 2008.

Gilly Sharpe — *Offending Girls: Young Women and Youth Justice*. New York: Routledge, 2012.

Randall G. Shelden — *Delinquency and Juvenile Justice in American Society*. Long Grove, IL: Waveland, 2006.

James F. Short Jr. and Lorine A. Hughes, eds. — *Studying Youth Gangs*. Lanham, MD: AltaMira Press, 2006.

Martin Stephenson — *Young People and Offending: Education, Youth Justice and Social Inclusion*. Portland, OR: Willan, 2007.

David Trend — *The Myth of Media Violence: A Critical Introduction*. Malden, MA: Blackwell, 2007.

Franklin E. Zimring — *American Juvenile Justice*. New York: Oxford University Press, 2005.

Index